Let the Scriptures Speak

Let the Scriptures Speak

Reflections on the Sunday Readings, Year C

Dennis Hamm, S.J.

A Liturgical Press Book

 THE LITURGICAL PRESS
Collegeville, Minnesota

www.litpress.org

Year B: ISBN 0-8146-2556-8
Year C: ISBN 0-8146-2557-6

1   2   3   4   5   6   7   8   9

Library of Congress Cataloging-in-Publication Data

Hamm, M. Dennis.
    Let the scriptures speak : reflections on the Sunday readings,
  year B / Dennis Hamm.
        p.   cm.
    Includes bibliographical references.
    ISBN 0-8146-2556-8 (alk. paper)
    1. Church year meditations.   2. Common lectionary—Meditations.
  3. Bible—Liturgical lessons, English—Meditations.   4. Catholic
  Church—Prayer-books and devotions—English.   I. Title.
  BX2170.C55H35   1999
  242'.3—dc21
                                                          99-19050
                                                             CIP

Contents

Introduction

For more than thirty years now, Catholics, as worshipers and preachers, have been stimulated and challenged in two ways by the renewal of the Service of the Word in our Eucharistic Liturgy. First, Vatican II mandated that the Lectionary should be revised so as to include a richer variety of biblical readings. Second, the council mandated that the sermon at Mass should be a biblical homily—an unfolding of Scripture, not simply a systematic exposition of doctrine or moral exhortation.

This enrichment of the liturgical readings and the mandate to preach more biblically has challenged us all. For preachers, it has meant a deeper and more constant study of Scripture. For all worshipers, as we were exposed to the greater variety of readings during the Service of the Word, it has called for greater attentiveness. And when preachers have mounted the podium without first immersing themselves in study of the biblical texts of the day, it has required tolerance and patience.

This situation has prompted the creation of many commentaries on the three cycles of Sunday readings. Some of these commentaries come in the form of homily helps, crib sheets for the harried pastor. Some of these helps expose each of the readings in an even-handed way, leaving the application to the preacher. Others provide a little background on the readings and then leap quickly to application. Some almost bypass commentary on the texts, move quickly to a vivid anecdote, and rush on to the application.

The reflections in this book take a different approach.

Realizing that the toughest challenge facing most of us, both as preachers and worshipers, is to hear the readings afresh and with understanding, my intent has been mainly to explain the readings. And since the three Sunday readings and their accompanying psalm offer more than one can fully absorb in one sitting, I have usually chosen to focus on one of the readings and then to refer to the others insofar as they complement what has caught my attention in the focus text. My first interest is in the meaning of the text in the context of the document, and in its original social context. For example, in explaining a passage from the letter to the Romans, I want first to hear what Paul meant by saying such a thing to that particular group of Christians gathered in that city at that time. My own experience is that the more I try to get at the meaning of the author, the easier it is to hear how those words can have meaning for us today.

When it comes to the readings from the Old Testament, I have tried to hear first the original meaning in the context of the Hebrew Scriptures and then to appreciate the Christian reinterpretation of the Jewish text. When it comes to contemporary application, I mainly hint and suggest, for two reasons: the limitations of space and the conviction that application is a very personal thing.

Knowing that one can no more write another's homilies than pray their prayers, I have been content to write explanations and reflections on the Sunday readings, in the hope that they will help others pray and preach.

Most of these reflections appeared first as the column called "The Word" occupying the final page of *America,* the U.S. Jesuit journal of opinion. They follow the readings of Year C of the Liturgical Year and appeared in the issues of *America* from November 22, 1997, through November 14, 1998. Quite naturally, they occasionally allude to current events during that period. Rather than delete these allusions or supply updated examples, I have let such references stand; usually the memories are still fresh and they often serve as reminders of other, more recent, parallels.

When I wrote these reflections for Year C in 1997–98, the feast of All Saints supplanted the 31st Sunday of the year. So I have written something for that Sunday, as well as one for the Nativity of John the Baptist (June 24th), which falls on a Sunday in 2001. As it happens, the first four Sundays of Lent happen to supplant the same four Sundays of the year as they did in 1998. That will not always be the case; so I have written fresh reflections for the 8th, 9th, 10th, and 11th Sundays in order that this series will fit any future occurrence of Year C. I have retained the All Saints reflection, along with three other date-linked solemnities—Mary, the Mother of God (Jan. 1) and the Epiphany of the Lord (Jan. 6), and All Saints (Nov. 1). (Those seeking ideas for five other date-linked solemnities—the Presentation of the Lord [Feb. 2], Saints Peter and Paul [June 29], the Transfiguration [Aug. 6], All Souls Day [Nov. 2], and the Dedication of the Lateran Basilica in Rome [Nov. 9]—will find these feasts treated in the Year B volume of this series.)

I owe special thanks to the editors of *America* for inviting me to write the reflections and to those readers whose positive feedback encouraged me to offer this material for publication as a collection. Thanks, too, to The Liturgical Press for electing to publish the columns as a set of three volumes, one for each cycle. I am especially grateful to Dr. Mary Kuhlman, whose alert eye and canny ear saved me countless times from infelicitous and obscure expression.

Dennis Hamm, S.J.
Creighton University

First Sunday of Advent

Readings: Jer 33:14-16; 1 Thess 3:12–4:2; Luke 21:25-28, 34-36

**"Beware that your hearts do not become drowsy from
carousing and drunkenness and the anxieties of daily
life, and that day catch you by surprise like a trap."
(Luke 21:34-35)**

BETWEEN TWO ADVENTS

What a difference a storm makes. I awoke this morning to see the deck railings outside my window sporting eight inches of wet snow. When I got out from under the covers, stood up in the chill of the room and looked out into the yard, I found that the same eight inches of snow had devastated our trees. Still fully in leaf after a moist and gentle fall, their branches had caught and held all that snow, and a third of the limbs had broken under the weight. Above them, other branches as yet unbroken swayed slowly under their burden like enormous heads of white elephants feeding on the chaos of vegetation strewn under their feet.

Over the radio came the news that fallen trees and branches had taken down power lines all over town, leaving fully 100,000 households without electric power. Somehow we on our hilltop were spared. Ready or not, storms come and do their thing. The poetry of apocalypse capitalizes on this fact of nature. Such imagery has more to do with vulnerability and unpredictability than with clues to the schedule of the coming end.

When Luke presents his version of Jesus' end-time discourse, he makes his own interpretive adjustments. Whereas Mark has Jesus speaking of the End to a private audience of four on Mount Olivet, Luke has Jesus speak these words publicly, in the Temple precincts. The king who must be about his Father's business has taken possession of the Temple area and has commenced teaching "all the people." Further, Luke has chosen to underscore the theme of the "time between"—what to do until the unpredictable End finally comes. Here, the destruction of the Temple (which did occur forty years after the crucifixion) is no longer closely linked to the Second Coming. Luke provides an ending that includes practical advice—the words quoted at the head of this reflection.

How do such words fit the First Sunday of Advent? Out of sync with every other time structure in our lives—the academic semester, the fiscal year, the twelve-month calendar, the cycle of the sports seasons—comes the beginning of the Church Year. That reminds us that we live out our faith lives in a time frame that is similarly "out of sync" with how most of the world calculates the movements of nature and history. Our "big picture" is anchored firmly between the first and second advents of Jesus Christ, Son of God and Son of Man. Just as we ended the Church Year with the theme of Christ the King of all kings, so we begin that liturgical cycle with the cosmic theme of the Second Coming that will complete the movement initiated by the first coming.

Meanwhile, Luke couches Jesus' advice for the "time between" in words very carefully chosen. "Beware that your hearts do not become drowsy [*barēthōsin*] . . ." The sense of that Greek verb is literally to be *weighed down;* Luke uses the same word to describe the numbed disciples at the Transfiguration, and in Matthew it describes the eyes of the disciples losing watchfulness in Gethsemane. And what causes this heaviness of heart? *Kraipalē,* "carousing and its result, hangover"—used only here in the New Testament. Another cause of that weighed-down heart is *merimnais biōtikais,* "biotic worries"—as in worrying about legal defense (Luke 12:11), or how to lengthen your life (Luke 12:25)—exactly the kind of thing that chokes the seed of the word of God and keeps it from maturing in one's life (Luke 8:14).

And what is the antidote to such numbness and drowsiness of heart? *Agrypneite,* "be watchful." Watchful for signs and cues regarding the end-time schedule? No. It is the watchfulness that accompanies prayer and leads to timely action.

Years ago—I think it was the summer the Gulf Coast was pounded by hurricane Camille—I recall reading a newspaper account about a group of people in Biloxi who disregarded calls to evacuate and chose instead to "ride out" the storm by having a party in their hotel room. The wind and waters came and took them under.

As we begin another Liturgical Year, the Church uses texts that call us to watchfulness. Jeremiah points to the time that has already begun, the first advent of the shoot of David who "shall do what is right and just in the land"—a coming we recognize as occurring two millennia ago. And the words of Paul to the Christians at Thessalonica look to the second advent when we will be present "before our God and Father at the coming of our Lord Jesus with all his holy ones." Paul says the best preparation for that advent is hearts strengthened through love of one another.

Second Sunday of Advent

Readings: Bar 5:1-9; Phil 1:4-6, 8-11; Luke 3:1-6

> **"'The winding roads shall be made straight,**
> **and the rough ways made smooth,**
> **and all flesh shall see the salvation of God.'"**
> **(Luke 3:5-6; Isa 40:5)**

THE INCARNATION, STILL DAWNING UPON US

Advent—what does it really mean for us? Are we pretending to get ready for something that we know has already happened? Are we rehearsing for a commemoration? Is it mainly about preparing for the biggest birthday party of all? Why then do the liturgical readings reach way ahead to the Second Coming?

Let me express a conviction straight out: Advent is about the incarnation. The enfleshment of the Eternal Word has indeed already occurred. In many ways, however, the Incarnation is still dawning on us, with all the connotations you can squeeze out of that word *dawning*—dawning in the sense of still unfolding its light against the dark, dawning in the sense of still edging into our awareness and understanding, dawning in the sense of still growing in our realization of its meaning and in its effect on our lives and on the world around us.

The broad sweep of that already-not-yet tension is abundantly present in the reading from Luke. Luke ushers John the Baptizer onto the stage in a way that connects both with the history of Israel and the sweep of the Roman Empire. Mark had already interpreted the Baptist's prophetic ministry with a line from Second Isaiah, "A voice of one crying out in the desert: / 'Prepare the way of the Lord, / make straight his paths'" (Mark 1:3, cf. Isa 40:3). When Isaiah spoke that verse during the Babylonian captivity, he was referring to the return of the Judean refugees to their homeland. And he celebrated that return using the imagery of a Near Eastern king moving in triumphant procession, his passage carefully prepared

3

with the filling of gullies and the rectifying of roads. For Isaiah, this home-coming was a new Exodus, a fresh liberating act of their saving God.

In applying this passage to John's preparation for Jesus, Mark was saying, What we have here is a *new* new Exodus. John was announcing the coming of Jesus, who would lead the people in a new freedom march. The way of life that Jesus would call the people to could be fittingly called "the way of the Lord"—"Lord" having become a proper title for Jesus, in the light of Easter.

As Luke saw things, Mark didn't know the half of it. Recognizing the rightness of Mark's application of Isaiah 40:3 to Jesus and his way, Luke realized there was much to be mined in that prophetic passage, namely the verses that followed the part cited by Mark, especially the part that runs "all flesh shall see the salvation of God." For in Luke's narrative Jesus will indeed bring sight to the blind, Paul will have his eye-opening experience on the road to Damascus, and Jesus, through the mission of his disciples, will be Isaiah's "light for the nations." The story of Jesus and the Church that Luke will tell in the Third Gospel and Acts will truly move in the direction of "all flesh" seeing the salvation of God.

Appropriately, then, Luke introduces John the way the Hebrew Bible introduces the prophets, with full a reference to who was in power at the time. Luke is careful to include the full list of Roman and Jewish officials in office at the time of John's debut and Jesus' movement from his hidden to his public life. Jesus' emergence in Israel, emphasized through a genealogy that stretches past Abraham back to Adam, has implications for everyone everywhere.

The passage from Baruch stands halfway between Isaiah and Luke. The author of that book, who honors Jeremiah's secretary by naming his scroll after him, writes after the return from the Exile. In the spirit of "Is that all there is? No, there's got to be more," he echoes Isaiah, using the very words our evangelists quote. He presents Lady Jerusalem using the image of a priest and envisions a future restoration of the people much greater than what they found after their return from exile.

When Paul, in the beginning of the letter to his beloved Philippians, utters a prayer of thanksgiving, he is the one in exile, in prison. And his focus is all on the glory of what is still just dawning in their lives as followers of Jesus. "I am confident of this, that the one who began the good work in you will continue to complete it until the day of Christ Jesus . . . And this is my prayer: that your love may increase ever more and more in knowledge and every kind of perception, to discern what is of value, so that you may be pure and blameless for the day of Christ. . . ."

Isaiah, Baruch, the Baptist, Mark, Luke—all together they prepare us to celebrate an incarnation still dawning on us.

Third Sunday of Advent

Readings: Zeph 3:14-18a; Phil 4:4-7; Luke 3:10-18

"Rejoice *(Gaudete)* in the Lord always,
I shall say it again: rejoice!" (Phil 4:4)

TOUGH JOY

How does anyone get away with *exhorting* others to rejoice? If you are feeling down, does it really help for someone to come along and say, "Cheer up"? And yet, without pausing to assess the mood and attitude of assembled worshipers, the Church makes bold to exhort people on the Third Sunday of Advent, ready or not, to rejoice. The tradition has its reasons, and the chosen texts are far more complex and challenging than any Pollyannish efforts to jump-start joy.

To make it perfectly clear that Advent is a preparation for the celebration of a gift that is, in great part, already realized, the Church punctuates this season with the joyful note of Gaudete Sunday, named after the Latin word heading the second reading, quoted above. (Laetare Sunday serves the same purpose during Lent.) Heard in context, the readings give sober, even hard-nosed reasons for joy.

Zephaniah prophesied early in the reign of Josiah, when hard things needed to be said regarding the religious chaos left from the previous administration of Manasseh. The part we read this Sunday comes from a hymn celebrating the survival of the faithful remnant, a passage that commentators judge was added after the Babylonian Captivity. It is sung, therefore, by a group that has passed through tough times. In the midst of those difficulties they have come to know the presence of God so vividly that they can picture the Lord "sing[ing] . . . as one sings at festivals." How did they get to be rejoicing survivors? In an earlier chapter the prophet had said, "Seek the LORD, all you humble of the earth, / who have observed his law; / Seek justice, seek humility; / perhaps you may be sheltered / on the day of the LORD's anger" (Zeph 2:3). This is not cheap joy.

When Paul exhorts his Philippians to rejoice, he is in a captivity of his own, in Roman custody while they try to figure out what kind of "king" and "kingdom" he is promoting on their turf. Like others who have been able to deal prayerfully with the enforced solitude of incarceration, he is able to urge rejoicing on much the same basis as Zephaniah's surviving Judahites: he has come to know the presence of the Lord. It is not wishful thinking but personal testimony that stands behind his pep talk: "Have no anxiety at all, but in everything, by prayer and petition, with thanksgiving, make your requests known to God. Then the peace of God that surpasses all understanding will guard your hearts and minds in Christ Jesus." Other imprisoned Christians, such as Dorothy Day and Martin Luther King, knew this; and so can we all, whatever the present challenge in our lives.

Climaxing these readings comes the episode from Luke, the prophetic challenge of John the Baptizer. I recall once seeing a smile light the faces of several more attentive congregants as they responded to the apparent irony of the final words of today's gospel reading: "'His winnowing fan is in his hand to clear his threshing floor and to gather the wheat into his barn, but the chaff he will burn with unquenchable fire.' Exhorting them in many other ways, he preached the good news to the people." On the face of it, the reference to burning with unquenchable fire did not sound like good news.

But that was Luke's word for it. Preaching good news was first of all Isaiah's way of talking about the coming of God in power, when "all flesh shall see the salvation of God." The Baptizer made it clear that the coming of God in the person of Jesus would mean good news to those whose lives were "fruitful" in ways that show repentance . . . and bad news to those whose lives did not produce such fruit. When questioned by the crowds as to what precisely "fruitful" living entailed, he replied concretely: don't cheat, don't extort, don't falsely accuse, be content with your wages, and share food and clothing.

And how is that good news? To paraphrase again: Under the reign of God, your life and what you do with it matter. Whatever your role—tax collector, soldier, butcher, baker—live it justly, and the world will be a better place and your destiny will be not the trash heap but the granary.

At the end of the day, the liturgy's exhortation to rejoice has little to do with mood and much to do with waking up to the good news of the incarnation. The way of life revealed in Jesus is both consoling and demanding. While most of us do not face exile or imprisonment, we do face the challenges of living justly and sharing with the needy—especially in the wake of an increasingly dismantled welfare system.

Fourth Sunday of Advent

Readings: Mic 5:1-4a; Heb 10:5-10; Luke 1:39-45

**"Sacrifice and offering you did not desire,
but a body you prepared for me."
(Heb 10:5b, quoting the Greek version of Psalm 40:7)**

OLD SONS, NEW KEY

If you want to get past the tinsel and ivy and the crush of shopping to recover the Christian meaning of the Birthday we approach, stop a moment and read Hebrews 10.

Most people, when they think of the relationship between the Old Testament and the New, account for that connection by referring vaguely to "promise and fulfillment"—as if it were simply a matter of prediction and occurrence. The reality is far more complex and interesting than that. The way the author of the letter to the Hebrews uses Psalm 40 to speak of the Incarnation is a stunning demonstration of how a Christian scribe brings from the storeroom of the Hebrew Scriptures "both the new and the old" (Matt 13:52).

The "something old" (and of continuing value) in Psalm 40 is its power as a prayer of thanksgiving for divine rescue and its claim that a heart obedient to God is a greater form of worship than temple sacrifices. The "something new" that the author of Hebrews finds there is how the psalm's words may be applied to the meaning of the life and death of Jesus.

A literal rendering of the Hebrew of Psalm 40:7 would be, "but ears you have dug for me." That is such a blunt image that most translations paraphrase, to clarify the apparent intent of the image, as in "but you have given me an open ear" (NRSV) or "but ears open to obedience you gave me" (NAB). The author of Hebrews uses the quite different Greek version, which reads "but a *body* you have *prepared* for me." Now Psalm 40 in *any* version works wonderfully as an interpretation of Jesus' person and mission; indeed, he taught that love of God and neighbor is worth more than all Temple sacrifices (Mark 12:33). But that Greek version, in what was the Bible of the early Church for the first three centuries, was a perfect vehicle for capturing the mystery of the incarnation—"a body you have prepared for me." For the human body in which the eternal Son becomes enfleshed is the means by which this representative of humanity can respond in perfect obedience to God. The atonement that temple sacrifices meant to accomplish finally reached fulfillment in the body of Jesus. In that body Jesus was able to live out a life and death that sealed the renewed covenant prophesied by Jeremiah 31.

Thus our author has found the perfect Christmas card in a Greek Psalm. Like the prologue of the Fourth Gospel and the "emptying-out" hymn of Philippians 2, the theologian of Hebrews cannot speak of the incarnation without moving to its climax in the paschal mystery. If that seems to collapse into a synthesis what the liturgical seasons are careful to sort out and separate, these texts remind us that the Liturgical Year is, after all, a way of moving through aspects of a single vision— how the Creator reveals and redeems in Christ Jesus.

Christmas Day

Readings: Isa 52:7-10; Heb 1:1-6; John 1:1-18

**"In times past, God spoke in partial and various ways
to our ancestors through the prophets; in these last
days, he has spoken to us through the Son, whom he
made heir of all things and through whom he created
the universe, who is the refulgence of his glory, the
very imprint of his being, and who sustains all things
by his mighty word. When he had accomplished purifi-
cation from sins, he took his seat at the right hand of
the Majesty on high, as far superior to the angels as the
name he has inherited is more excellent than theirs."
(Heb 1:1-4)**

MORE OLD SONGS RE-KEYED

The introduction to the letter to the Hebrews, taken from the second
reading this Christmas, is quoted above in full to help you see readily
how the writer's reading of Psalm 40 is already expressed in the prologue. Incarnation leads to redemption. And both are the fullness of
the Creator's Self-communication. What the Creator spoke through
nature and through prophets, he expressed even more fully and effec-
tively through the humanity of Jesus. Just as on Sunday we saw this
author find christology in Psalm 40, so in the rest of this reading he
plays Old Testament texts in a new key to proclaim the incarnation.
Psalm 2:7 ("You are my son; this day I have begotten you"), originally
referring to the accession of a Hebrew king, now preaches Jesus. And
so it continues with 2 Samuel 7:14, Deuteronomy 32:43, and Psalms
104, 45, 102, and 110, singing old songs in a new key. Open your Bible
to Hebrews 1 and unpack these treasures for yourself.

Holy Family of Jesus, Mary, and Joseph

Readings: 1 Sam 1:20-22, 24-28; Col 3:12-17; Luke 2:41-52

> **"He said to them, . . . 'Did you not know that I had to be in my Father's house [NAB, NIB; 'about my Father's business,' KJV, Rheims]?' But they did not understand what he said to them." (Luke 2:49)**

The Open Family

As I was driving to Des Moines, Iowa, to give a workshop, the voice on NPR let me know that I was heading for what was, at that moment, the most famous town on earth—the place where Bobbi and Kenny McCaughey had just become the parents of seven children. The four boys and three girls, though in delicate condition because of their prematurity, were all well formed and their prospects good. The public response was vigorous and various. Some imagined the scenario of 35,000 diaper changes before toilet training took effect. Others focused on clinical dimensions: "For the average consumer it will obscure the downside [of multiple pregnancy]," observed one physician. What came through loud and clear was Bobbi's pro-life choice when the plurality of her pregnancy had been discovered. Presented with the option to "reduce the number of fetuses" in order to avoid the real risk of losing all, she chose to gamble on God. Led by her faith that all life is a gift from God, she chose to carry all seven to term.

In one sense, this sevenfold wonder simply dramatized what is a fact of normal life: *any* family, even a single mother with one child, participates in a mystery involving them intimately with the Creator and imposes more responsibilities than any of us can fully comprehend and adequately carry out alone.

Luke, in the seventh scene of his introduction to the public life of Jesus, presents an abundant reminder of these dimensions of family and parenting. The account of Jesus lost and found in the Temple is as much a story of the parents as of the child. Mary and Joseph are returning from Jerusalem, having completed the annual pilgrimage to the Holy City for the celebration of Passover. Assuming that twelve-year-old Jesus is safe somewhere in the caravan of relatives and friends (no smothering over-protectiveness here), they are surprised, after a day's journey, to discover that the child is not among them. Finally, after three days of searching for him "with great anxiety," Jesus confronts them with a statement that would carry little consolation for any parent: "Why did you search for me? Did you not know I had to be *en tois tou patros mou?*" I quote those last words in Luke's Greek because it is one of those places where the Third Evangelist seems deliberately to be using ambiguous language. A literal rendering would be "in the [things] of my Father," which commentators have mainly taken to mean "about the affairs of my father" (referring to action) or "in the house of my father" (referring to a place). The mysterious openness of the phrase leaves one thing crystal clear, Jesus' life involves an obedience to more than earthly parents. Mary has just referred to Joseph as Jesus' father, but Jesus uses the word *patēr* of the Creator. Yet, Luke hastens to show that doing the will of his heavenly Father entailed obedience to Mary and Joseph: "He went down with them, and came to Nazareth, and was obedient to them."

As exceptional as these things may be—the birth of septuplets and the unique family relationships of Jesus—both the Des Moines story and the Lucan episode remind us that being family is an intimate involvement with the divine—more challenging than we expect, more promising than we could hope for. And we always need outside help.

Mary, the Mother of God, and the Naming of Jesus

Readings: Num 6:22-27; Gal 4:4-7; Luke 2:16-21

"When the fullness of time had come, God sent his Son, born of a woman, born under the law, to ransom those under the law, so that we might receive adoption."
(Gal 4:4-5)

WHO'S A CHILD OF GOD?

True or false?—According the Bible, every human being is a child of God. False. What the Bible says about *everybody* is that we are *created in the image* of God (which should be enough to motivate people of biblical faith to work toward a universal respect for all members of the human family). But the Bible reserves parent-child talk, first, for the relationship of God and the people of Israel (in those places, like Exodus 4:23 and Hosea 11:1, where Israel as a whole is designated "son" of God). Then, in the New Testament "sonship" is a special language used for Christians, male and female. The second reading for today is a case in point.

Paul, writing to the (largely Gentile) Christians of Galatia, reminds them that the divine Son, born of the Jewish woman Miriam enabled all of them, men and women alike, to share in the sonship of Jesus (in whom there is neither Jew nor Greek, neither male nor female [Gal 3:28]). The adoption language used of Israel in its relationship to God is now boldly applied to those baptized into the body of Christ; there, "the Spirit of God's Son" enables the baptized to know themselves as children of God by addressing the Creator of the cosmos as *Abba* ("Father").

That use of children-of-God language regarding Christians might at first seem limiting and exclusive, but consider Stanley Hauerwas' modest proposal—that Christians resolve not to kill other Christians.

Think of the difference such an attitude might have made in the story of Europe, and in the recent histories of Ruwanda and Northern Ireland. If Christians fully recognized one another as adopted children of God, we might more easily recognize the image of God in the rest of the human race. At least it is a place to start.

Epiphany of the Lord

Readings: Isa 60:1-6; Eph 3:2-3a, 5-6; Matt 2:1-12

> **"Nations shall walk by your light,**
> **and kings by your shining radiance."**
> **(Isa 60:3)**

Lumen Gentium

The prophet that we call Third Isaiah, writing after the return of the Judeans to their homeland from Babylon, looks ahead to a time of even further restoration, when Zion would so reflect the light of God that the nations would flock to it. It is a renewal of the vision expressed long before by First Isaiah, picturing a time when all nations would stream toward Jerusalem to learn Torah and beat swords into plowshares (Isa 2:2-5). Further, today's reading echoes the songs of Second Isaiah, who envisioned Servant Israel missioned as a "light to the nations." Matthew's account of the Magi worshiping the child Jesus reflects the early Church's conviction that the Christ's coming began to fulfill that vision of Isaiah. When the authors of Vatican II chose the phrase *Lumen gentium* to name the Dogmatic Constitution of the Church, they meant to remind us that the vision of the People of God as a "light for the nations" still beckons.

Second Sunday after Christmas

Readings: Sir 24:1-2, 8-12; Eph 1:3-6, 15-18; John 1:1-18

> "And the Word became flesh
> and made his dwelling among us,
> and we saw his glory,
> the glory as of the Father's only Son,
> full of grace and truth."
> **(John 1:14)**

WISDOM PITCHED HER TENT WITH US IN JESUS

Against the all too human desire always to dash after something new, St. Ignatius, in his *Spiritual Exercises,* urges repetition. When you have found something in your prayer that moves you, he advises, stay with it and go deeper. Soak it up. When you think of it, repetition is pretty human too. Children like nothing better than hearing a story they love told over and over again. The same holds true of our favorite dishes from mother's cooking. Well, the readings for the second Sunday after Christmas call us to that same kind of savory repetition. We hear the same Gospel we heard on Christmas morning, the Prologue of John's Gospel. But this time we hear it against the background of a different set or prior readings, enabling us to hear the familiar words accompanied with new resonances. The evangelist himself draws on that passage from Sirach 24 when he composes what may be the most influential sentence in Christian thought and worship, verse 14, quoted at the head of this reflection.

Sirach 24 portrays the wisdom of God personified as a woman who speaks of her presence first in the Wilderness tent amidst wandering Israel, then later in the Temple of Jerusalem. Wisdom personified is a way of speaking of divine presence, active in a special way among the chosen people. That way of picturing God's presence, of course, made perfect sense to Israel even before the Christian experience. The Israelites had learned a special way of relating to the presence of God in the sacred space and ritual of the Temple.

It is a breathtaking leap, then, when John asserts in his hymn that this Wisdom of God—which he describes as the eternal *logos,* or Word—*tented* in a whole new and intimate way in the humanity of Jesus of Nazareth. The word behind the translation "made his dwelling"—*eskēnōsen*—actually has the root meaning "tented." This comes through later in Jesus' reference to the "temple of his body" in John 2:21. What a powerful way to describe the incarnation—the divine Wisdom tenting among us in the humanity of Jesus.

The sentence continues with further allusions to the Hebrew Scriptures. When John says, "we saw his glory," this is not some fuzzy reference to greatness or splendor. "Glory" carried a specific biblical denotation; "glory," translating *kebod* (literally, "heavy" in a connotation oddly close to the sense that word had in American slang in the '60s) meant a physical manifestation of the presence of God, especially as that was experienced in the Temple liturgy. This association allows John again to say something powerful about the incarnation: the fullness of the physical manifestation of the presence of God is . . . the humanity of Jesus of Nazareth.

But there is even more to this rich sentence. John says further that the manifestation of the divine in Jesus is "full of grace and truth." This phrase, too, comes bearing Old Testament echoes. "Grace and truth" is a consecrated phrase in the Hebrew Bible for describing the covenant love of God. In other words, all that was manifested and experienced in Israel's covenant relationship with the Lord God is now expressed in an ultimate way in the Word and Wisdom of God made flesh in Jesus of Nazareth.

Having led us through the celebration of the birth of Jesus, the mystery of the Holy Family, the motherhood of Mary, and the Epiphany, the Church, on this second Sunday after Christmas, calls us to a contemplative "repetition." Hearing the prologue of John against the background of Woman Wisdom's song in Sirach 24, we can rest for a moment in the sheer wonder of the incarnation. In this contemplation, the words from the second reading (Ephesians) are a most appropriate blessing: "May the eyes of your hearts be enlightened, that you may know what is the hope that belongs to his call, what are the riches of glory in his inheritance among the holy ones" (Eph 1:18).

Baptism of the Lord

Readings: Isa 42:1-4, 6-7; Acts 10:34-38; Luke 3:15-16, 21-22

> **"After all the people had been baptized and Jesus also
> had been baptized and was praying, heaven was
> opened and the Holy Spirit descended upon him in
> bodily form like a dove. And a voice came from heaven,
> 'You are my beloved Son; with you I am well pleased.'"**
> **(Luke 3:21-22)**

INSPIRED HINDSIGHT

Ask your parents how they met. If you haven't heard it already, you will likely hear a treasured story about an event which may have seemed quite ordinary at the time. Maybe the meeting was a function of sharing the same part of the alphabet and therefore being seated next to each other in math class. Hindsight reveals a seemingly trivial encounter to have been momentous—momentous for your parents (whose lives might otherwise have gone separate ways) but even more momentous for you (without that meeting, you would likely not have come into existence).

The baptism of Jesus at the Jordan may have been like that. The crowd of Judeans submitting themselves to John's immersion ritual may not have taken much notice of the Galilean in their midst. But all the evangelists, drawing on the hindsight of the Church's reflection, agree that this event at the Jordan was a profoundly significant moment—in the history of Israel, in the story of Jesus, and in the lives of his followers.

Luke's two-verse account is packed with clues to the larger meanings of this inaugural event. First, Luke passes over the action of John. Luke simply says that *after* everyone, including Jesus, had been baptized, Jesus *was praying*. Already Luke has made two important interpretive moves: (1) Jesus is in the midst of "all the people," thereby invoking an important theme in the Third Gospel, Jesus' solidarity with the people of Israel; (2) Jesus' being at prayer prepares us for the other times in Luke and Acts when prayer and empowerment by the Holy Spirit are linked—in the instruction on prayer (Luke 11:13), the choosing of the Twelve (Luke 6:12 with Acts 1:2), and Pentecost (Acts 1–2).

When he speaks of the descent of the Holy Spirit upon Jesus, Luke is careful to add the phrase "in bodily form" because the attentive reader of his gospel will remember that Jesus was already announced as *conceived* by the Holy Spirit (1:35); and so this experience of the Holy Spirit is not something unprecedented in Jesus' life but a fresh manifestation of a relationship already established.

As for the statement of the divine voice from heaven, Luke leaves Mark's version untouched, for it carries a fullness that cannot be improved. "You are my beloved Son" bears a double resonance. First, it evokes the heavenly voice quoted in Psalm 2:7 announcing the accession of a divinely appointed king, therefore a messianic sonship. Second, the phrase "beloved son" recalls to Jewish ears the famous place in the Torah where that phrase occurs as a kind of refrain (three times, in Gen 22:2, 12, and 16). This is the Akedah, the Binding of Isaac. Thus the emergence of Jesus into his public ministry is announced in language that already hints the end of that life on Calvary.

Finally, "with you I am well pleased" echoes Isaiah 42:1, the beginning of the first Servant Song of Isaiah, this Sunday's first reading. That simple phrase, then, recalls the whole mission sketched by that song: bringing forth justice to the nations with the gentleness that refrains from breaking the bruised reed, bringing light to the blind and freeing prisoners.

Thus in two short verses inspired hindsight presents the emergence of Jesus into his public life in a way that shows him to be Messiah of Israel, Son of God, and Prophet to the nations. The Old Testament background clarifies why the Church sees our own baptism as an immersion into that same mission.

Second Sunday of the Year

Readings: Isa 62:1-5; 1 Cor 12:4-11; John 2:1-11

"Jesus did this as the beginning of his signs in Cana in Galilee and so revealed his glory. . . ." (John 2:11)

THE BRIDEGROOM IS HERE

The metaphor of marriage imaging God's relationship with the people of God is deep in the Hebrew Bible. Yahweh is to Israel as husband is to wife. Think of Hosea's comparison of his troubled marriage with the story of God's relationship with Israel. The oracles of Isaiah use this tradition with regard to Israel's future (even messianic) restoration, as for example in this Sunday's first reading, where the coming vindication of Jerusalem is portrayed as a wedding feast for God and his spouse (a sexual image that resists any effort to render it gender-neutral).

Jesus himself makes bold to apply the tradition to himself. When the Pharisees ask why Jesus' disciples are not into extra fasting like those of the Baptist (Mark 2:18), he replies, "Can the wedding guests fast while the bridegroom is with them?" He continues the metaphor by speaking of his presence and ministry as "new wine" demanding new wineskins.

This background helps us appreciate the account of the wedding feast of Cana. Far more is going on here than an affirmation that Jesus "liked a good party" or was affirming the institution of marriage. Both are surely true. But in the Fourth Evangelist's framework, the wedding feast at Cana is nothing less than the revelation of divinity in Jesus as Word made flesh.

John states that the wedding at Cana occurred "on the third day." Third day relative to what? Relative to Exodus 19:11 and 16, as it turns out. For in the account of Yahweh's appearance on Mount Sinai at the giving of the covenant (Exodus 19–24), the appearance occurs on the third day, and it is twice referred to as a display of God's "glory" (24:16-17). John's account of the wedding begins with the third-day note and ends by saying that by this sign Jesus "revealed his glory." These connections would not be lost on readers who knew their Torah and only moments before had read the prologue, which includes such claims as "The Word became flesh . . . and we saw his glory . . . full of grace and truth. . . . From his fullness we have all received, grace in place of grace, because while the law was given through Moses, grace and truth came through Jesus Christ" (1:14, 16).

Cana, in a sense, acts this out. Take the jars of water become wine. One hundred twenty to one hundred eighty gallons of wine is a lot of wine. And John is careful to note that the containers are stone jars, that is, vases not made the usual ceramic way, out of clay worked and baked, but sculpted out blocks of stone. Such jars were costly, the very best, and always pure because they were nonporous. John notes that there are six and that they are there for the purpose of Jewish ritual washing. The symbolism is clear. As stone and large, they are special and abundant; but as only six (not seven), they are incomplete. When people do what Jesus says, water becomes a surprising abundance of the best wine of all. The bridegroom has arrived with new wine. The wedding party of the new covenant has begun.

Third Sunday of the Year

Readings: Neh 8:2-4a, 5-6, 8-10; 1 Cor 12:12-30; Luke 1:1-4; 4:14-21

> **"All in the synagogue had their eyes fixed on him. Then
> he began by saying to them, 'Today this Scripture
> passage is fulfilled in your hearing.'" (Luke 4:20-21)**

SCRIPTURE ON SCRIPTURE

It happens all the time. Jews do it. Muslims do it. Christians do it. A group of people, gathered to worship the living God, have someone read to them from an old book. Their reasons are the same: the ancient writings speak of how their ancestors in the faith experienced the One who started and sustains the world and who took initiatives to make them a people. Further, they acknowledge that they are still in living relationship with that God, who deserves their thanks, listens and responds to their petitions, and takes profound interest in what they do with their lives. People read the old book to know who they are and what they are doing.

The first and third readings for this Sunday highlight that recurring situation. We have the priest Ezra, addressing the people of Judah some eighty years after the return from the Babylonian captivity, still working to restore a common life around a reconstructed Temple and Holy City. He is reading an updated version of the people's constitution—the Law, or Torah. In the Gospel reading we hear the voice of Luke himself introducing his version of the story of Jesus, a fresh edition required by the community of his day (which will include a "part two"—the Acts of the Apostles—telling the story of the early Church). Further, one of the episodes Luke chooses for special treatment is the scene of Jesus' homecoming in the synagogue of Nazareth, where Jesus himself, paralleling Ezra, reads from Scripture and asserts its relevance for "today"—the present moment of his community of listeners, and, for Luke, the present moment of his readers, then and now.

This is one of those occasions when Scripture speaks of Scripture, when the Bible becomes a kind of user's manual about itself.

The scene in Luke is stunning. A well-known member of this small village (population, archeologists estimate, around 150), the town bachelor and craftsman, returns with a reputation for healing and acting like an old-time prophet. He shows up at the synagogue, opens the scroll of Isaiah to the place we call chapter 61, reads the first-person statement of a prophetic figure claiming to be anointed and sent by the Lord for a work of liberation and healing, and boldly applies that passage to himself.

Thus Ezra, Jesus, and Luke—each in his own way shows us what our Bible reading at liturgy is all about: we read the ancient writings because they speak to us of our relationship to God and to one another—*today*.

Then there is the passage from Paul. He wrote a letter addressing the needs of a particular Greek community in the 50s of the first century. The unity of the Christian community in Corinth was threatened in several ways—by rivalries, by dualistic thinking, by neglect of the poor. Paul responded to this particular set of crises so eloquently that this "occasional" letter eventually became recognized as inspired Scripture, capable of addressing any community, any time, about the essentials of Christian unity.

In the passage read today, we hear the famous body image. The life of the Spirit that the Church shares makes it an organism analogous to any other living body. Like the limbs and organs of a human body, the members of the body of Christ (the Church) each have a special and needed role to play, whose purpose is to build up that body. Apart from that body, the particular member is as significant as a 165-pound eye sitting in the grass, splendid to behold but connected to nothing.

Paul's image of Church as body helps us think about the Church's current call for a "preferential option for the poor." That is a reflection of what happens in nature all the time. Recently, for example, when I had an infected thumbnail, my body spontaneously and consistently *favored* that small member; I didn't have to be persuaded to make a "preferential option" for my thumb. If we are tempted, in the context of both Church and state, to neglect the poor among us, it may be because we have lost touch with the ways in which we are in fact one body. Restoring the sense of connection may have something to do with the mission of liberation and healing that Jesus would continue through us.

Thus Paul joins Ezra (and the Chronicler who writes of Ezra), Jesus, and Luke in teaching us why we read old writings when we gather to worship (even at times when "Water Gate" [Neh 8:1] does not have a special, accidental, resonance).

Fourth Sunday of the Year

Readings: Jer 1:4-5, 17-19; 1 Cor 12:31–13:13; Luke 4:21-30

> **"If I have the gift of prophecy . . . but have not love,**
> **I am nothing." (1 Cor 13:2)**

Who's a Prophet?

We are rightly suspicious of self-appointed prophets. Biblical warrant for this suspicion lies in the fact that the typical prophet in Scripture is profoundly reluctant to accept the appointment. Whence the sarcastic label "self-anointed prophet" applied to anyone who too readily claims such a role. In most biblical contexts, the term *prophet* means "forth-teller" rather than "fore-teller." That is, the designated person is asked to speak to the community in the name of God. Sometimes, indeed, the message does include reference to the future, but mainly it is a message the community needs to hear regarding how it ought to alter its way of proceeding in the present.

In our appropriate restraint to name or claim to be prophets, we more readily apply the term to dead messengers (Martin Luther King, Pope John XXIII, Dorothy Day) than to living ones (Sister Helen Prejean?—one of my candidates). And yet, our Scriptures invite us to take the role of prophet with utmost seriousness—regarding Jesus, the apostles, and ourselves. Jeremiah was for the early Church the archetypal prophet, so much so that language from his call story (this Sunday's first reading) is used to describe our archetypal apostle, St. Paul; he uses Jeremiah's call to describe his own vocation (Gal 1:15), and Luke does the same in Acts 26:17. The Gospel reading shows Jesus placing his mission in the prophetic tradition of Elijah and Elisha. Further, our theology of baptism describes our own Christian mission as a participation in Jesus' role of prophet, along with the awesome roles of priest and king.

What can give perspective to any application of the role of prophet to ourselves or others is Paul's reflection on the place of *love* as the "way" of exercising all the gifts. When we feel called to confront our little part of the world in the name of God—that is, according to an informed conscience—it must be motivated by love. Otherwise our action is empty and our perceived role self-appointed.

Fifth Sunday of the Year

Readings: Isa 6:1-2b, 3-8; 1 Cor 15:1-11; Luke 5:1-11

> **"Then I heard the voice of the Lord saying, 'Whom shall I send? Who will go for us?' 'Here I am,' I said; 'send me!'" (Isa 6:8)**

GETTING SENT

Isaiah in the Temple, Peter in the fishing boat, and Paul writing to his beloved Corinthians—what do they have in common? Each of this Sunday's three readings reflects on their experience of being commissioned as servants of God. As different as these three situations are—a Hebrew prophet in the Solomonic Temple, a Galilean fisherman surprised by an enormous catch, and a Greek-writing Pharisee reflecting on being a Christian convert—the three scenarios have startlingly similar elements.

Each of these men is confronted by an awesome manifestation of divine power. Isaiah of Jerusalem has a vision that he can only call "seeing the Lord." Celestial beings called Seraphim (literally "burning ones") sing the praise that we have incorporated into our Eucharistic Prayer: "Holy, holy, holy is the LORD of hosts! All the earth is filled with his glory!" Thus the prophet comes to know God, not just as a local Near Eastern divinity but as the God of all, the One whose glory is shown in all creation. This becomes a major theme for this prophet and the successors who speak in his name: Yahweh, the creator of all, is the redeemer of Israel.

For Peter, the awesome manifestation of the divine comes in the form of an amazingly abundant catch after a night of fruitless toil. As in the wine-sign at Cana, a surprising abundance follows obedient response to the command of Jesus.

For Paul, pondering his place in the transmission of the Gospel message, the awesome experience was a vision of Jesus as risen Lord on the road to Damascus ("Last of all, as to one born abnormally, he appeared to me"). As it was with Isaiah, Paul encounters an unbidden divine vision.

In the presence of the divine manifestation, all three feel a profound unworthiness. "Woe is me," says Isaiah. "I am doomed! For I am a man of unclean lips, living among a people of unclean lips; yet my eyes have seen the King, the LORD of Hosts!" Peter's reaction to the titanic catch is to fall at Jesus' knees and say, "Depart from me, Lord, for I am a sinful man." As for Paul, when he reflects on his experience, he can only say, "I am the least of the apostles, not fit to be called an apostle, because I persecuted the church of God."

In each case, what followed that sense of unworthiness was a divine assurance and—the biggest surprise of all—a commission. One of the "burning ones" touches Isaiah with an ember and assures him that his wickedness is purged. Then the future prophet hears the voice of the Lord asking for a volunteer. The amazed and kneeling Peter hears Jesus address him, "Do not be afraid; from now on you will be catching men." For his part, Paul found himself drawn into a mission of surprising fruitfulness (amazingly effective among Gentiles rather than among his fellow Jews). When he alludes to this mission as he writes to the Corinthians, he is compelled to say, "But by the grace of God I am what I am, and his grace to me has not been ineffective. Indeed, I have toiled harder than all of them; not I, however, but the grace of God that is with me."

Clearly, in this pattern of the calls of Isaiah, Peter, and Paul, there is a message for all of us. We who find ourselves blessed with a sense of divine presence inevitably feel a sense of unworthiness in proportion to our sense of God's goodness. But God does not allow us to stay there. Along comes the purifying ember (God healing in us what we are unable to fix) and then some sense of a task, as if to say: "Forget about your unworthiness, I have a job for you to do; get up and do what needs to be done, and I'll see that you get the support you need."

What does it take to be ready for the divine manifestation in the first place? Isaiah was worshiping in the Temple. Peter was plying his trade and alert to the Master's suggestion. And Paul, even as he was persecuting what he later recognized to be "the church of God," was following his best lights, zealous for God.

The systematic theology of grace and human freedom may be complicated, but these call stories give us all the ingredients.

Sixth Sunday of the Year

Readings: Jer 17:5-8; 1 Cor 15:12, 16-20; Luke 6:20-26

**"Blessed are you who are poor,
for the kingdom of God is yours." (Luke 6:20)**

ASHES OR WATER—YOUR MOVE

A colleague reports the following exchange with a New York cabby. When the driver asked my friend the reason for his visit, he told of attending a convention in which they analyzed ethical dilemmas illustrated by case histories. "Yeah," mused the cabby. "Sometimes you just gotta forget your principles and do what's right."

Why is that so funny? I submit that the humor comes lies in the absurdity of knowing "what's right" apart from some principles. At the same time, the comment recognizes that our sense of what is right springs from something deeper than our articulated principles can express. This Sunday's readings point in that direction. The images of the bush and the tree in Jeremiah 17 illustrate two basic orientations possible in the living of a human life—no matter what one's career or lifestyle. One can either "seek . . . strength in flesh"—that is, put one's trust in one's own power or the merely human, ignoring the divine source of one's being—or one can trust and hope in the Lord. The former, or "flesh," orientation will lead to a life of sterility with "no change of season," whereas the latter orientation (trusting the Lord) will lead to a life of fearlessness and fruitfulness. (St. Paul names those two orientations "walking in the flesh" and "walking in the spirit.")

Jeremiah's powerfully imaged set of alternatives provide a perfect preparation for hearing Luke's version of the Beatitudes. Notice that Luke's Beatitudes differ from the more familiar eight (nine, really) Beatitudes in Matthew in that the Third Gospel presents them in a set of four blessings paralleled by a contrasting set of four woes. In Luke's version, Jesus first congratulates those who are poor, hungry, weeping and excluded, and he issues woes to those who are rich, full, laughing, and well thought of.

When Jesus blesses the poor and curses the rich, is he congratulating the economically deprived and condemning those with ample possessions? Although many argue that Matthew's "poor in spirit" dilutes Luke's "poor," there is a growing consensus that by "poor" Jesus means not a social class but those who know their need for God. Of course, it frequently happens that those who feel the pinch of poverty have a lively sense of their need for God, whereas the affluent, with needs well provided for, often become numb to their need for God. Hearing Luke's blessings and woes after Jeremiah's picture of the sterile bush and the fertile tree can help us see that Jesus' pointed contrast presents not two situations but two orientations—Jeremiah's "flesh [self] or God."

Seventh Sunday of the Year

Readings: 1 Sam 26:2, 7-9, 12-13, 22-23; 1 Cor 15:45-49;
Luke 6:27-38

"Be merciful, just as your Father is merciful." (Luke 6:36)

CREATIVE NONVIOLENCE

David as teacher of nonviolence? In the full flush of his power as king, David will show himself capable of murder in the service of lust. Desiring Bathsheba, he will arrange for her husband Uriah to die in combat. But the writer of the royal history takes delight in showing that this same man is capable of remarkable acts of what we today have learned to call creative (even playful) nonviolence.

Two stunning examples of this behavior occur during Saul's search-and-destroy mission against the pre-monarchic David. The first happens while David is hiding in a cave at Engedi. When Saul enters that cave to relieve himself, David sneaks up behind and cuts off the end of his mantle. Then David reveals himself to his would-be killer, letting Saul know that he had refrained from taking advantage of his vulnerability: "Since I cut off an end of your mantle and did not kill you, see and be convinced that I plan no harm and no rebellion. I have done you no wrong, though you are hunting me down to take my life. The Lord will judge between me and you . . . ."

We find a similar example in today's first reading. Saul continues his pursuit of David into the desert of Ziph. One night David and Abishai are able to steal into Saul's barricade to the place where the king and his general are sleeping. David declines Abishai's offer to nail Saul to the ground "with one thrust of the spear." Instead, he delicately refrains from harming his enemy and makes off with the king's spear and water jug. From a safe distance, David taunts Abner and Saul and shames the king into a change of heart.

Charmed and perhaps even inspired by these nonviolent strategies of David, we come to the Gospel passage, the core of Luke's Sermon on the Plain, with fresh ears. What David did occasionally as a clever ploy, Jesus of Nazareth expands into a way of life. Nonviolence sits at the heart of Jesus' teaching. There can be no doubt that Matthew and Luke understood it that way. Matthew, in his presentation of Jesus' teaching in the Sermon on the Mount, places the sayings about nonviolence and love of enemies as the climactic elements of the famous six antitheses of chapter 5. In his much shorter version of that sermon, Luke gives love of enemies an even higher profile: he places the mandates of enemy-love and nonviolence immediately after the Beatitudes and Woes. Six verses later, Luke rounds off that passage by repeating the mandate.

When it comes to the motivation for nonviolence, David and Jesus have more in common than may at first be apparent. David's moves are more than crafty strategies of self-protection. He deals with his enemy as a fellow human being under the judgment of God. ("Today, though the LORD delivered you into my grasp, I would not harm the LORD's anointed.") And when Jesus of Nazareth commands nonviolence and love of enemies, he urges as his rationale nothing less than the *imitation of God!* (". . . you will be children of the Most High, for he himself is kind to the ungrateful and the wicked.") This sums up a rationale spelled out more completely in Matthew's version: "But I say to you love your enemies . . . that you may be children of your heavenly Father, for he makes his sun rise on the bad and good, and causes rain to fall on the just and the unjust" (5:45). In other words, be as inclusive in your benevolence as the Creator.

Where Matthew summarizes this attitude as a matter of perfection—"Be perfect, just as your heavenly Father is perfect" (5:48)—Luke records the more appealing (and, scholars think, the more original) version of the saying: "Be merciful, just as your Father is merciful." The word translated "merciful" is a rare word, *oiktirmōn*, used only here in the Gospels (and elsewhere in the New Testament, only at James 5:11, where the author is echoing Old Testament characterizations of God such as Exod 34:6 and Ps 103:8). It refers to the covenant love of the Creator of all. We who claim to know God in that way are mandated to extend that mercy to all.

Christian love of enemies, and consequent nonviolence, is not something we do simply by willing it; it springs from a relationship with God and the covenant community. And yet it is a mandate.

A question to ponder: the two Gospel sermons presenting the inaugural teaching of Jesus make nonviolence and love of enemies central to that teaching. Why has our Christian teaching and practice been so slow to recognize this? To make it concrete, which is closer to the teaching of Jesus: the death penalty, or life imprisonment without possibility of parole?

First Sunday of Lent

Readings: Deut 26:4-10; Rom 10:8-13; Luke 4:1-13

> **"The devil said to him, 'If you are the Son of God,**
> **command this stone to become bread.' Jesus answered**
> **him, 'It is written, *One does not live on bread alone.'"***
> **(Luke 4:3-4 [Deut 8:3])**

THE TESTING OF JESUS (AND ISRAEL AND US)

A ritual offering of the first fruits and the diabolic testing of Jesus in the desert—what possible connection could there be between these two scenarios? Actually, the connection is profound and well worth pondering.

Deuteronomy 26 is one of the best places in the Bible to get an insight into the point and power of a simple religious ritual. Put yourself in the sandals of an Israelite of the late seventh century B.C.E. and ask yourself what you would be doing if you were carrying out the ritual expressed in these instructions. You would have gathered a basketful of the first fruits of the harvest—wheat, say, or barley—and you would be bringing it up to the Jerusalem Temple to present before one of the priests on duty. As you offer the basket, you say, "Today I acknowledge to the LORD, my God, that I have indeed come into the land which he swore to our fathers he would give us" (Deut 26:3).

This is a six-century flashback. You are a descendant of Israelites who came into the land many generations ago. In this single gesture you are acknowledging that the very soil you farm is a gift of God in two ways. First, as creator God made the earth and sustains its power to produce food in the form of plants; second, as the redeemer of Israel from slavery in Egypt, God gave you the land as a place to live in freedom. In one gesture you confess Yahweh as the God of nature (versus the baals of the Canaanites) and the Lord of history, the one who liberated and sustained your nation against its enemies. All this is summarized in the story of the Exodus that you recite in the "credo" of the next nine verses. Finally, you link that story to your ritual gesture in the final words of your prayer: "Therefore, I have now brought you the first fruits of the products of the soil which you, O LORD, have given me" (v. 10). Then you "make merry over all these good things which the LORD, your God, has given you" (26:11).

This is what I mean by the genius of the ritual: in one action, with a few well chosen words, you worship God as God of nature (creator) and Lord of history (redeemer). Notice that this ritual and creed caps the presentation of the Deuteronomic Code (Deut 12–25), which spells out the covenant relationships between Israel and God. The ritual gesture underscores the foundation of those relationships in the initiatives of God as creator and redeemer.

When we come to the account of the testing of Jesus after forty days of fasting in the desert, we find that we are still in the ambiance of the book of Deuteronomy. Not only do the "forty days" recall the "forty years" of Israel's sojourn in the wilderness. All three of Jesus' responses to the devil's temptations are drawn from that story of Israel's testing in the desert (God's testing of Israel and Israel's testing of God) as told in Deuteronomy 6 through 8.

When the devil challenges Jesus to demonstrate his divine sonship by commanding stones to turn into bread, Jesus quotes Deuteronomy 8:3, "One does not live on bread alone"—which those who knew their Deuteronomy would complete with the words, "but by every word that comes from the mouth of the LORD." When the devil offers Jesus all the kingdoms of the world if Jesus would worship him, Jesus paraphrases Deuteronomy 6:13, "You shall worship the Lord your God; him alone shall you serve." When the devil shifts from temptations to arrogance to a temptation to presumption (if you are the Son of God, jump from the Temple parapet; God will surely protect you), Jesus quotes Deuteronomy 6:16, "You shall not put the Lord, your God, to the test." Once we are in touch with the context of Deuteronomy, it becomes clear that Jesus is here pictured as reliving the story of Israel in the wilderness, and getting it right. The parallel (and contrast) extends even to the talk of sonship: "So you must realize that the LORD, your God, disciplines you even as a man disciplines his son" (Deut 8:5).

What is conveyed in the ritual of Deuteronomy 26 and in the testing account of Luke 4 is reflected powerfully in every eucharistic celebration. In the Offertory we bring to the priest bread and wine, "fruit of the earth and work of human hands"—much like the Israelite enacting Deuteronomy 26. Then, in the blessing of the sacrament the fruits of the earth become the body and blood of the obedient Son, with whose self-giving sacrifice we identify as we join the Son's act of worship of the Father. Christian worship has not left behind the genius of its Israelite roots.

Second Sunday of Lent

Readings: Gen 15:5-12, 17-18; Phil 3:17–4:1; Luke 9:28b-36

"But our citizenship is in heaven, and from it we also await a savior, the Lord Jesus Christ." (Phil 3:20)

SEEING THINGS

"You're *seeing* things!" Any lifelong speaker of American English will hear in that phrase a judgment that the person addressed is out of touch, imagining what is not really there. But here I want to give that phrase a little spin to help us reflect that faith is, in a positive way, always a matter of *seeing things* in a way that is not universally shared. Each of this Sunday's readings illustrates that fact.

Abram, a senior citizen and husband of a woman well past menopause, is told to look up at the stars and believe that, sterility notwithstanding, he and Sarah shall have descendants as numerous as those stars. Abram puts his faith in the Lord, who credits it to him as an act of righteousness. To confirm this promise, the Lord has Abram lay out some split animal carcasses to set up for a covenant ritual in which the two covenanting parties walk between the pieces as a sign of their commitment. The meaning of the ritual: if I fail in this agreement, may I suffer the fate of these animals. Then Abram sees a smoking brazier and a flaming torch pass between the pieces—symbolizing, in an unusual gesture of divine condescension, God's commitment to the promise. Because he allows himself to see the future God's way, with fertility coming out of sterility, God lets him really see things—a vision confirming the divine promise.

When Paul writes to his beloved Christian community in the Roman colony of Philippi, he calls them more deeply into the Christian way of seeing things. They have a mindset, a worldview, different from the culture around them. For those other folks, "their God is their stomach; . . . . Their minds are occupied with earthly things." "But our citizenship is in heaven," he tells them, touching on a reality that is very much a part of their daily experience. For they are citizens of a Roman *colonia*. As Christians, however, they are a colony of heaven, members of a homeland whose shores they have not touched, yet whose citizens they already are. By embracing the risen Lord in faith, they can look forward to becoming transformed and sharing in his risen state. They envision a future that frees them even now.

In the Gospel reading, Jesus takes Peter, James, and John up a mountain to pray. There they experience a vision even more dramatic than that given to Abram. Jesus' face and clothing are transformed into an apocalyptic brilliance. Moses and Elijah join Jesus "in glory" and speak with him. Peter wants somehow to "freeze" the scenario by setting up three tents. Then—in a way that recalls the divine presence overshadowing the wilderness tent of meeting (Exod 40:34-35) and the Solomonic Temple at its dedication (1 Kgs 8:10)—a cloud overshadows them all. Moses and Elijah fade; the three see "only Jesus." Then the same divine voice that spoke at the baptism of Jesus announces, "This is my chosen Son; listen to him."

What Peter, James, and John are seeing they don't fully grasp until their understanding is illuminated by the light of Easter. We have the advantage of Luke's post-Easter hindsight as we read his account. Luke alone stresses that the vision occurs while Jesus and the privileged three are praying. And Luke alone notes that the subject of Moses' and Elijah's conversation with Jesus is "the *exodus* he is to fulfill in Jerusalem." The mention of that key word is a powerful shorthand interpretation of Jesus' coming death and resurrection: what looks to be a crushing disaster will turn out to be the occasion of a liberation journey of which the first exodus is a foreshadowing. For the vision's Jewish viewers—Peter, James, and John—the presence of Moses and Elijah necessarily recalls the Law and the Prophets. For Moses is the mediator of the Sinai covenant and the leader of the Exodus, and Elijah is the prophet par excellence and the hoped-for precursor of the messianic age. Thus these figures stand for the essence of God's communication with Israel. And so, when Moses and Elijah fade and Jesus alone remains visible and the divine voice says, "This is my chosen Son; listen to *him*," the message is clear: Jesus, in his Easter "Exodus," is the fullness of God's word. He fulfills the Law and the Prophets.

It is no accident that the evangelists link this vision with the teaching on discipleship immediately preceding it. Jesus had been teaching, "Whoever wishes to save his life will lose it, but whoever loses his life for my sake will save it" (9:24). The vision of the Transfiguration hints how such a paradox can be true. This Gospel vision reminds us that we too are meant to be "seeing things" as we move through our lenten journey.

Third Sunday of Lent

Readings: Exod 3:1-8a, 13-15; 1 Cor 10:1-6, 10-12; Luke 13:1-9

"As he looked on, he was surprised to see that the bush, though on fire, was not consumed." (Exod 3:2b)

BURNING BUSH, BARREN FIG TREE

If there is a "Top 10" list of Bible passages conveying the essence of the Jewish and Christian idea of God, the one about Moses and the burning bush is surely included.

Consider how the mystery of divine presence is conveyed. As in the theophanies experienced by Abram and Gideon, the text refers to that presence by shifting among several names—"the angel of the Lord," "God," "the Lord." Though the narrator first speaks of a messenger (angel), and Moses sees fire, it is clear that Moses knows he is dealing with God ("Moses hid his face, for he was afraid to look at God," v. 6). This dramatizes the insight that our human experience of God is always somehow distinct from God.

Then there is the paradox of the fire that burns the bush without consuming it. What better way to portray the intense presence of Creator to creature? Now more than ever, we know that our cosmos is literally enlivened by fire, the relationship of planet Earth to the Sun being our own best example. Similarly, the reflection of Christian philosophy treasures the insight that all beings derive their existence from the One who is not another being but Being itself (something that Exodus 3 makes explicit). In that sense, every creature is a kind of burning bush whose existence is fired by God without being consumed. The nonconsumption hints that the sustaining Presence can be intimately present without violating the distinct essence of the creature.

If such considerations seem more philosophical than Hebrew poetry warrants, consider the conversation about the name of the Presence. Although we read three names for the Presence—*malach YHWH* ("an angel of the Lord"), *YHWH* ("the Lord") and *Elohim* ("God")—Moses asks to know the name of the One who is commissioning him. He is told, "I am who am." Then God adds, "This is what you shall tell the Israelites: I AM sent me to you." This is an unpacking of the divine name, YHWH. That most famous of four-letter words remained, in the Jewish tradition, a name too sacred to be pronounced (expect for once a year, on Atonement Day, by the high priest). To this day, when a Jewish reader comes to the Hebrew letters transliterated as YHWH, he or she says the substitute name *Adonai* ("the Lord"). This practice has been enshrined in most translations. The Jerusalem Bible broke with the tradition by rendering *YHWH* as "Yahweh," which we Christians now boldly sing in some of our hymns. (The nonbiblical name "Jehovah" results from the misguided combination of the vowels of *Adonai* with the consonants *YHWH*.)

As mentioned above, that mysterious name "I am who am [Greek, *egō eimi ho ōn;* Latin, *ego sum qui est*]" became a catalyst for the Christian metaphysics of creation—the cosmos as beings sustained by the Creator who is pure Being. But finally the account is not about metaphysical speculation; it is about the love of this mysterious Presence who intervenes to rescue through human agency. Caught up simultaneously in the *attraction* and *fear* that Rudolph Otto identified as primary ingredients *(fascinans et tremendum)* of religious experience, Moses is commissioned to do something in the name of the God of his ancestors. The Creator does not simply sustain (which would be plenty!). The Creator redeems, frees Israel from bondage, with a little help from such diffident souls as Moses.

In the Gospel reading, we hear Jesus draw on another image for the divine/human interaction: a fruitless fig tree. Whereas Mark (and Matthew following him) had told of Jesus' performing the prophetic *action* of cursing a fruitless fig tree (standing for the unproductive religious leadership of Israel), Luke clarifies this confusing action by presenting it as a *parable* (Luke 13:6-9) of a fruitless fig tree. Here we cannot doubt that the tree is symbolic. It stands for everyone who hears Jesus' call for repentance. The fruitlessness signifies the life lived out of touch with God. The way to fruitfulness is turning the heart to its source, the One who is.

Paul, writing to his Corinthians, conveys the same note of urgency. If the very people who experienced God's liberating power in the Exodus could lose their sense of the divine presence sustaining and saving them, it behooves those of us who claim to have entered "the end of the ages" in Christ not to remain complacent. In our own wilderness trek, we are subject to our own addictions and idolatries. The call to attend to the divine presence and respond is still urgent. Lent is for responding to that call. The One Who Is would enlist us in his saving work.

Fourth Sunday of Lent

Readings: Josh 5:9a, 10-12; 2 Cor 5:17-21; Luke 15:1-3, 11-32

"And all this is from God, who has reconciled us to himself through Christ and given us the ministry of reconciliation . . ." (2 Cor 5:18)

THE MINISTRY OF RECONCILIATION

Ask ten people to tell the story of the prodigal son, and chances are that eight or nine of them will manage to retrieve the basic plot. It is, after all, one of the best-known stories in the world. But ask those same ten people, "On what occasion did Jesus tell that story?" and it is unlikely that any of them will know. The story is so powerful and clear that it has taken on a life of its own. Yet Luke was very careful to provide a definite setting for the story in his Gospel. Attending to that context discloses further depths in an already deeply meaningful parable.

Luke establishes the setting in a single sentence. "The tax collectors and sinners were all drawing near to listen to him, but the Pharisees and scribes began to complain, saying, 'This man welcomes sinners and eats with them'" (Luke 15:1-2). This critique recalls the scene in Luke 5:27-32, Levi's dinner party, where the Pharisees and their scribes raise the same complaint, and Jesus replies, "Those who are healthy do not need a physician, but the sick do. I have not come to call the righteous to repentance but sinners."

The sentence beginning today's reading evokes the same scene and issue. Again Jesus responds with a defense of his table fellowship with the outcast—only this time his strategy is storytelling. He begins with two similitudes, parables that base their comparison on a recurring social situation. The first is the one about the shepherd going after the lost sheep; the second, the one about the woman searching for a treasured lost coin. The point of each image is double-edged: edge no. 1, the shepherd and the woman both picture the divine attitude of care for the repentant sinner; edge no. 2, the rejoicing in each similitude represents Jesus' own table fellowship with (repentant) tax collectors and sinners.

Finally, to drive his point home, Jesus follows these stories of the lost sheep and the lost coin with his story of the two lost sons. Yes, we find that the famous "Prodigal Son" story comes as the climax in a series of three, all in the same setting. Familiar as it is, the parable is full of surprises if we take it slowly, attending to the details.

The first surprise is a shocker: the younger son dares to ask his father for his inheritance—"pre-posthumously!"—an intolerably dishonorable request in that, or any, culture.

Second surprise: the elder son says nothing.

Third surprise: the father actually goes along with the idea and divides the property between the two sons.

Fourth surprise: the younger son turns the property into liquid capital, departs, and shoots the whole wad in Gentile territory, where he is reduced to tending pigs and nearly starving.

Fifth surprise: when the runaway returns with a plan to relate to his family as a salaried worker, his father welcomes him back with multiple signs of full reconciliation: the father's own festal robe, the family signet ring, and sandals—clearly marking him as family as distinguished from the (barefoot) servants.

Sixth surprise: the father ensures reconciliation with the whole village by throwing a huge party around a roasted fatted calf.

Surprise number seven is the one experienced by the elder son when he returns from the field to discover this unscheduled party celebrating his wastrel brother's return. His reaction is bitter: "All these years I slaved for you and never disobeyed one of your commandments" (a literal rendering of the Greek).

Notice what happens when we hear all this in Luke's setting, Jesus defending his inclusive table fellowship against the charges of the scribes and Pharisees. In the portraits of the runaway and the compassionate father, the tax collectors and sinners hear a confirmation of the reconciliation they have found in Jesus' ministry to them. Whereas the scribes and Pharisees are invited to contemplate an image of themselves in the cartoon figure of the elder son, who has completely misread his filial relationship as one of slavery—a clear parody of their misguided sense of religion.

When Paul writes to the competitive Corinthians that God, who has reconciled us to himself through Christ, has given us a ministry of reconciliation, he is clearly calling all Christians to that same ministry. If we find ourselves resonating with bitterness of the elder son, we have some repentance to do.

Fifth Sunday of Lent

Readings: Isa 43:16-21; Phil 3:8-14; John 8:1-11

> **"Remember not the events of the past,**
> **the things of long ago consider not;**
> **see, I am doing something new!" (Isa 43:18-19)**

STUNNING THE STONERS

How does it happen that a group of men catch a woman "in the very act" of committing adultery, and only the woman is apprehended? What happened to her partner? Was he too fast for the witnesses? Already the scenario is suspect. And if the scribes and Pharisees are bent on justice, why do they bring the alleged adulteress to Jesus rather than to one of their legal officials? They refer to the fact that the Law of Moses mandates the death penalty in such a case and ask what Jesus has to say. Has Jesus developed the reputation of being "soft" on offenders and they hope to catch him in violation of the Torah by pleading for her pardon?

The Evangelist says, "They said this to test him, so that they could have some charge to bring against him." What is the test? If, as some scholars think, the Roman government had taken from the Sanhedrin the right of capital punishment, then Jesus' questioners may think they are putting Jesus in a no-win situation. On the one hand, if he advocates stoning, he puts himself at odds with the Roman officials, who no longer permit such activity. On the other hand, if he advocates that she not be stoned, he would appear to deny the law of Moses and thereby put himself in a bad light with Jewish officials.

Jesus refuses to play his adversaries' game. Instead, he proceeds to do that famously enigmatic writing on the ground. It is attractive to think that Jesus' gesture may be an allusion to Jeremiah 17:13: "Those who turn away from thee shall be written in the earth, for they have forsaken the Lord, the fountain of living water"—but that is simply one guess among many possibilities. What the narrative makes clear is that Jesus refuses to be lured into their trap. When they continue to press him, Jesus says, "Let the one among you who is without sin be the first to throw a stone at her."

Is Jesus suggesting that the criminal law and legal punishment can only be administered by sinless people? That would be a remarkably unrealistic proposal. And such an abstract principle hardly seems to be the issue here. Is not the point, rather, that the Pharisees' present activity of manipulating this woman and setting up a "sting operation" for Jesus is itself sinful behavior? Appearing to be seekers after law and order, they are exposed as hypocrites simply bent on protecting their own power. Jesus' delay tactic of scribbling on the ground has allowed some time for this reality to sink in. One by one, the accusers depart, leaving Jesus alone with the accused.

In words that suggest that he is savoring the irony of the situation, Jesus says, "Woman, where are they? Has no one condemned you?" "No one, sir," she says. Then Jesus says, "Neither do I condemn you. Go, and from now on do not sin any more." What delicacy. As every preacher has observed, Jesus forgives the sinner without denying the sin. Mercy invites conversion.

The readings from Isaiah and Paul help us savor more deeply what we witness in this encounter between Jesus, his testers, and the woman. Even though the passage from Second Isaiah was, first of all, addressed to the refugees in Babylon and speaks of the good news of their freedom to journey home to Judah under the liberation of Cyrus, the words have come to mean much more. First Jews, then Christians, came to read these words, like most of Isaiah 40–55, as descriptions on the messianic times. The Church applies to the new Exodus of incarnation and redemption in Jesus the words, "See, I am doing something new!" And we dare to hear as addressed to ourselves the words, "the people whom I formed for myself, that they might announce my praise."

Paul, writing to the Philippians about the legalistic teachers who would impose the fullness of Jewish tradition and practice upon Christian Gentiles, insists on the newness that faith in Jesus has brought into his life as a keeper of the Torah. We have no reason to suspect that Paul denigrates the Law or his own Jewishness; it is simply that he finds in Jesus such an illumination of the Law and the Prophets, that he has come to know that his relationship with God comes from God and not from his own achievement. Like the woman caught in adultery, Paul has discovered himself on the receiving end of a divine love that enables him to live the law in love.

Although Jesus makes no general commentary on the death penalty in today's passage, the "something new" that he brought into the world has led the Church in our own day to seriously challenge capital punishment—whether by stoning, hanging, gas, poison, or electric shock—as a moral means for pursuing justice and protecting the common good.

Passion (Palm) Sunday

Readings: Luke 19:28-40; Isa 50:4-7; Phil 2:6-11; Luke 22:14–23:56

> "They proclaimed,
> 'Blessed is the king who comes
> in the name of the Lord.'" (Luke 19:38)

NOTES FOR PASSION SUNDAY

Passion Week commences with this Sunday's commemoration of the entry into Jerusalem and the reading of the Passion according to St. Luke. It is a time when the pageantry and the texts are so rich that there is little call for a full-bodied homily. It is usually enough for the preacher to help those assembled to focus on the ironies of the palm branches and the donkey (see last year's [Year B] commentary for this Sunday). It can also be helpful to take a moment before the reading of the passion to attend to some of the nuances that make Luke's account of Jesus' final days distinctive. Here are a few details worth prayerful attention.

In his rendition of the Last Supper, Luke, alone among the Synoptic writers, includes a repetition of the argument among the disciples about which of them should be regarded as the greatest (23:24 = 9:46). He then presents Jesus' teaching on how Christian service should contrast with Gentile authoritarianism—a teaching that, in Mark, followed the third passion prediction. Why does Luke go out of his way to repeat the embarrassing spectacle of apostolic ambition—right in the middle of the Last Supper? And why does he postpone to this occasion the teaching on the service entailed in discipleship? The most likely explanation is that the evangelist wants to bring home to his readers that, for a community formed by the Eucharist, competition for preference is a scandal and mutual service is a mandate.

It is Luke who calls Jesus' experience in Gethsemane an *agōnia*, which may carry the older meaning of "fight" or "combat." For in Luke's version, the "grief" that Mark ascribes to Jesus is here transferred to the disciples, and instead of shuttling between his solitary, anxious prayer and his disciples and falling prostrate, here Jesus kneels down, once, and prays simply (again, just once): "Father, if you are willing, take this cup away from me; still, not my will but yours be done." Luke has chosen to underscore Jesus' decisive confrontation in prayer both with "the cup" and his own resistance to it.

The Jewish leaders stress political elements in their charges: Jesus is fomenting a tax revolt, is claiming to be a king, and stirs up the people from Galilee to Judea. Pilate declares Jesus innocent of any capital crime, a verdict that is echoed by the centurion under the cross who says, "Truly this man was *dikaios*," which means both "righteous" (i.e., a keeper of all the covenant relationships) and "innocent" (in the forensic sense); both surely apply here.

It is Luke's version of the crucifixion and death that gives us Jesus' remarkable expression of forgiveness: "Father, forgive them; they know not what they do." For all of us who are challenged by this radical modeling of love of enemies, it is helpful to note that Jesus' statement is a prayer. Whatever may have been Jesus' interior readiness to forgive, the fact that it is expressed as a prayer of petition gives a helpful option to followers of Jesus who find forgiveness of unrepentant adversaries next to impossible. What may not come spontaneously from the human heart can be requested in prayer.

The mocking of Jesus' messiahship is shared evenly between the (Jewish) rulers and the (Roman) soldiers. They taunt the messiah and king to save himself—at which point Luke notes the assertion of the mutely articulate sign, "This is the king of the Jews."

Luke's version is unique in showing the two crucified bandits picking up that royal theme, each in his own way. One of them can only echo the taunt of rulers, "Are you not the Christ? Save yourself and us." But the other turns the theme into an act of faith, "Jesus, remember me when you come into your kingdom." Then Jesus, staying with the king theme, responds, "Amen, I say to you, today you will be with me in *Paradise*" (a Persian loan-word meaning "the king's garden").

Luke omits the famous cry of dereliction—"My God, my God, why have you forsaken me?"—the only words we hear from the cross in Mark and Matthew. Instead he records, "Father, into your hands I commend my spirit." Both sayings are quotations from Psalms. The first is the opening of Psalm 22, which moves from a sense of abandonment to a strong hope for vindication. The second is from Psalm 31, which also has the same movement, with the advantage of including the powerful expression of confidence carried in the quoted verse. Thus Luke helps us understand that Jesus' own experience and prayer could move from the darkness of near-despair to the light of complete trust in the Father.

Easter Sunday

Readings: Acts 10:34a, 37-43; 1 Cor 5:6b-8; John 20:1-9

"Then Peter proceeded to speak and said, 'In truth, I see that God shows no partiality.'" (Acts 10:34-35)

PETER ON EVANGELIZING

For those who first encountered it, the empty tomb was a shock. The phrase death-and-resurrection flows so smoothly from our lips that we can easily miss the fact that, whatever Jesus may have said about his vindication after death, his followers were as unprepared for the enigma of the empty tomb as they had been for the scandal of crucifixion.

Luke speaks of the apostles' initial dismissal of the women's testimony and of the Emmaus disciples' puzzlement (Luke 24:10, 22). And John, in this Sunday's Gospel reading, presents another version of that same experience. Mary Magdalene's first instinct upon seeing the stone rolled away from the tomb entrance is to bolt. She runs to Peter and the beloved disciple and reports that the body has been removed.

Why the puzzlement? Whatever Jesus had said about resurrection (and in John's Gospel Jesus utters three mysterious sayings about being "lifted up"—usually taken as a reference to both crucifixion and resurrection), clearly none of the disciples (except "the beloved disciple") was prepared to understand. In the prevalent Jewish understanding, the resurrection of the dead was something that happened not to a single individual but to the whole community, and at the end-time. For most of Jesus' disciples, it took an appearance of the risen Lord to impress them with the reality of Jesus' glorification. The surprise was twofold: one person had indeed been raised from the dead and, yes, the expected end-times had begun to unfold. It would take some weeks for the realization of this to dawn fully; but soon this frightened and confused group would become a joyful community with a clear mission to continue the preaching and healing of their risen Lord.

We get a glimpse of the fuller understanding in the reading from Acts. Here Luke gives us Peter's speech to the centurion Cornelius and his household. This is the first example in Acts of preaching to a non-Jewish audience. Curiously, the Lectionary drops the speech's expansive first sentence: "In truth, I see that God shows no partiality. Rather, in every nation whoever fears him and acts uprightly is acceptable to him"—omitted perhaps because it requires the context to make complete sense. The previous part of the chapter (Acts 10) had told how it took a series of divine interventions (visions to both Peter and Cornelius and an embassy from Caesarea to Joppa) to overcome Peter's reluctance to extend the mission to Gentiles. Already a "God fearer"—that is, a Gentile who has adopted Jewish faith and prayer—Cornelius tells Peter about his own visionary experience and says, "We are all here in the presence of God to listen to all that you have been commanded by the Lord" (10:33).

This whole episode, and the speech that crystallizes it, provides a wealth of insights for the Church's current focus on evangelization.

Evangelization is first God's work. Peter can describe the whole of Jesus' ministry as a matter of God "evangelizing peace through Jesus Christ." It is noteworthy that Luke's word here is *euangelizomenos,* the same Greek word from which we get "evangelizing"—which Luke himself apparently got from Isaiah (see Isa 52:7, which refers to spreading the good news of redemption from captivity as "evangelizing peace").

Evangelization presumes God's universal salvific will. "In every nation whoever fears him and acts uprightly is acceptable to him" (10:35).

God's plan for evangelization exceeds our own preconceptions. Peter had to be divinely stretched beyond his own limited notion of the mission.

Evangelization is mainly storytelling and witnessing in a situation of hospitality. To a group of people who are ready to hear it, Peter tells of his experience of God in Jesus of Nazareth. This creates the occasion for the listeners to receive the gift of faith.

The Good News of Jesus "healing the oppressed," leading to a death and vindicated by resurrection is at the core of the message shared.

Evangelization is also a summons to conversion. The promise of forgiveness entails the admission of sinfulness. The risen Lord will judge the living and the dead.

Evangelization itself is not an "extra" but a divine mandate. "He commissioned us to preach to the people" (v. 42).

And so Magdalene's surprise and Peter's speech both help us learn about our own call to share the Good News that springs from Easter.

Second Sunday of Easter

Readings: Acts 5:12-16; Rev 1:9-11a, 12-13, 17-19; John 20:19-31

**"But these are written that you may come to believe
that Jesus is the Christ, the Son of God, and that
through this belief you may have life in his name."
(John 20:31)**

DISTRESS, KINGDOM, AND ENDURANCE

As we enter this third millennium, fundamentalist preachers continue to find explicit predictions of the future in the Christian Apocalypse. Scholars, meanwhile, continue to remind us that this strange book has more to say about the past than about the future—with some encouraging but not particularly newsy implications for the present. So let us approach with care and intelligence this Sunday's reading from the inaugural vision of the book of Revelation.

John—apparently not the Baptist or the Evangelist but another John, whom we can call the seer—first tells how he wound up in a Roman penal colony. He was jailed for evangelizing, probably by Roman officials who found his message a threat to the emperor worship deemed necessary for law and order in their district. He celebrates the fact that he shares with his readers "the distress, the kingdom, and the endurance we have in Jesus." Those few words epitomize the message of the whole work.

"The distress" refers to the hostility of much of the Roman world about them, especially the pressure to compromise their faith by participating in emperor worship.

"The kingdom," of course, refers to the kingdom of God—the reign of God preached by Jesus and now experienced by his followers in the Christian communities flowering around the eastern end of the empire. Apocalypses, from Daniel forward, were always about power, asserting that, no matter how much it seems that some earthly tyrant is in power (be it Nebuchadnezzar, Antiochus IV, or some Caesar), the real king of the universe is Yahweh. Now that reign (or kingdom) comes through the rule of the lamb that was slain, the risen Jesus.

That reign is the source of the Christian power to "endure." The knowledge that the world is ultimately governed and judged by the One, the sevenfold Spirit, and the Lamb enables Christians to endure any temporary despot the world can enthrone. The next twenty-one chapters unfold that message. The inaugural vision of the risen Jesus—along with the seven messages and the heavenly vision that follow—sets the stage.

In an image from Daniel 7, Jesus is described as "one like a son of man" (who in Daniel's vision, after the judgment of history's abusive empires, receives "dominion, glory, and kingship" over all nations—Dan 7:14). The ankle-length robe suggests his role as priest, for the risen Jesus is the ultimate mediator of atonement for the community. The gold sash around his chest, clearly a regal accessory, signifies his kingship.

The detail that the hair on his head was white as wool or snow is missing from our Lectionary, probably judged by an editor as oddly distracting. But it is part of the cluster of images from Daniel 7 applied to Jesus, and therefore not hard to understand. For in Daniel's vision it is "the Ancient One"—YHWH—who is described as having wool-white hair as he sits in judgment on the nations. Ascribing to the risen Jesus that feature associated in Daniel with the divine judge is a robust affirmation of the divinity of Christ. In short, all the details that may strike the uninstructed twenty-first-century reader as simply weird were comforting reminders to the first-century audience of familiar realities of their faith: no matter what earthly power seems to be in charge, the risen Lord has the fullness of power and will, in time, have the final word.

Thus the point of the Christian apocalypse is to remind a harassed readership that the Lord is in charge. The point of Christian apocalypse is to realize that our hope in a just future is rooted in the past victory of the Lamb that was slain and raised in glory. The remainder of Revelation is a set of variations on that simple, ever valid, theme.

The other two readings picture the effects of the Lord's victory in other contexts. The vignette of Acts 5 completes Luke's summary description of life in the early postresurrection community. They continue the preaching and healing ministry of Jesus, spontaneously share their material possessions to meet the needs of all, and "many signs and wonders were done among the people at the hands of the apostles." In the Gospel, the struggle of Thomas to believe that the Lord has risen prompts a statement addressed to us all: "Blessed are those who have not seen and have believed." John the seer expresses in apocalyptic form the same faith embodied in the community of Acts and in the apostle Thomas. All three help us face the present with a hope based solidly on the great event of our past—the Easter victory of the Lamb.

Third Sunday of Easter

Readings: Acts 5:27b-32, 40b-41; Rev 5:11-14; John 21:1-19

> **"But Peter and the apostles said in reply,
> 'We must obey God rather than men.'" (Acts 5:29)**

RADICAL OBEDIENCE

I recall the advice of an older pastor to a young assistant, "One thing you must never do: never ask people to choose between their country and their church."

This Sunday's reading from Acts seems to pose that kind of radical alternative. Peter and John are arrested, hauled before the Sanhedrin, and ordered to cease preaching in the name of Jesus. In response to this expression of the highest authority in their Jewish lives, they assert boldly, "We must obey God rather than men."

That episode has become a classic text supporting Christian resistance to misguided authority. When human lawgivers contradict divine law, the faithful are to resist, obeying God—as their conscience, formed by the community, leads them to hear God's will. Does this vision of Christian resistance to erring or unjust authority present precisely the awful choice warned against by the pastor's statement quoted above? Only rarely, it seems to me. What this passage suggests, in our situation as U.S. Catholics today, is our call to be vigilant and active citizens. We are rarely, if ever, faced with that either/or choice of Church versus country. True patriotism requires that we participate in our democratic system in ways that sometimes challenge laws and public policy in order to heal and improve the life of our nation (the commonweal, to use a venerable word).

Our immigrant forebears were necessarily preoccupied with building an alternative school system, enabling Catholics to keep the faith as they worked to enter the mainstream, and proving that Catholics could be good citizens who offered no threat of some clandestine Roman takeover. That task accomplished, we are now in a position to help *shape* the mainstream of our culture with the humane vision of

Catholic social teaching—a vision of the common good that challenges *both* of our political parties.

Even in those cases when the consciences of some call them to conscientious objection and even civil disobedience, the presumption is that we do these things within the setting of our legal system, and with the intention of making that system more just. This is not a matter of Church versus state. Indeed, we serve our nation best when our primary effort is to obey our God. That obedience can help overcome our selfishness and enable us to look beyond our vested interests and attend to the common good.

We need not reach far to recall how the U.S. Church has heard and responded to the call to obey God rather than men. For example, our Church leadership has rallied us to oppose the practice of abortion, even as our highest court has sanctioned it. Our Pope and our bishops have strongly opposed the death penalty, even as most of our states continue to mandate it. Our Pope and our bishops opposed the use of military force in the Middle East at the time of "Desert Storm" and in the current crisis with Iraq, even as our nation worked to rally the U.N. to such a military effort. Our U.S. bishops, in their pastoral letters on peace (1983) and economic justice (1986), dared to teach that our faith vision provides the basis for critiquing and challenging military and economic policy and for seeing that Christian discipleship and citizenship are intimately connected.

Two charcoal fires burn in the Fourth Gospel. The first warms Peter in Caiaphus's courtyard when, as predicted, he denies his master three times. Today's Gospel presents the other charcoal fire, near which Jesus invites the denier to atone for his cowardice by confessing his love three times. Each time Jesus asks Peter to demonstrate that love by service: "Feed my sheep, my lambs." He then predicts that Peter's service will take him where he does not want to go. The Church's social justice ministry is an important form of that pastoral service. And, yes, sometimes that ministry takes us where we do not instinctively want to go.

The scene from Revelation 5 presents every creature in the universe praising and honoring the risen Lamb that was slain. This is a healthy reminder that our own service of that Lamb involves a living out of his teaching regarding love of enemies, meeting the needs of all, and the nonviolent resolution of conflict. The Easter victory of that Lamb can, if we allow it, energize us as it did the apostles.

Taking a stand for the unborn, the displaced, the downsized, the harassed, the "disappeared," the overlooked, the hungry, the homeless—these things will sometimes take us where we do not want to go and find us "worthy to suffer dishonor," but done in the spirit of the risen Jesus, they lead to rejoicing.

Fourth Sunday of Easter

Readings: Acts 13:14, 43-52; Rev 7:9, 14b-17; John 10:27-30

"For so the Lord has commanded us, *I have made you a light to the Gentiles, that you may be an instrument of salvation to the ends of the earth.*" (Acts 13:47; Isa 49:6)

Visions And Revisions

The language can sound so otherworldly—eternal life, the multitude gathered around the lamb on the throne praising him day and night. Such talk seems to be vulnerable to the secularist's mocking use of the phrase "pie in the sky by and by" to satirize a perceived Christian pre-occupation with the next world. Well, of course there *is* a next world, and resurrection faith helps keep that reality alive for us. But a careful hearing of this Sunday's readings soon brings us back to earth, with our feet firmly planted on the ground and with a strong sense of direction.

First, the vision of Revelation 7 comes as part of a remarkable *re*-vision. In the first half of this chapter, the seer had spoken of an audition (that's right, an *audition*, something heard rather than seen) of 144,000 people, comprising 12,000 "from every tribe of the Israelites." The enumeration of the "servants of our God" comes across as a rather specific census, so specific in fact that the passage has spooked some Christians into thinking that the number of those who experience salvation will be limited precisely to 144,000.

But this audition is immediately followed by a *vision* (something seen) of "a great multitude, *which no one could count,* from every nation, race, people, and tongue. They stood before the throne and before the Lamb, wearing white robes and holding palm branches in their hands." Thus we have an audition about a numbered group (144,000) of Israelites and a vision about a numberless group of people from every nation. Are these two groups? No. They are two presentations of the same group. The audition announces them as the end-time Israel, which was a common early Christian way of referring to the Church. And the vision presents them in more literal terms (but with a literary allusion to the language of Daniel 7), as an enormous group including all nations and races. This double-take of the same subject should not surprise the careful reader, who would already have encountered the same phenomenon in chapter 5, in a similar audition/vision sequence where the risen Jesus is first announced as "the lion of the tribe of Judah" and then appears as "a lamb, that seemed to have been slain" (vv. 5-6). Attention to this set of images should expand considerably most Christians' sense of God's plan of salvation. It also reminds us that in our Easter joy we rally around a crucified Messiah who was a scandal to the Jews and foolishness to the Greeks.

A similar revision of vision occurs in the Gospel. Jesus' statement about giving eternal life to his sheep occurs at a celebration of the feast of Dedication, i.e., Hanukkah, which commemorates the Maccabees' successful revolution against the Syrian tyrant Antiochus IV around 194 B.C.E. The evangelist says some of the people celebrating that feast were asking Jesus whether he was the Messiah. The context suggests that they were thinking of a Messiah along the militaristic lines of David the warrior and the Judah the Hammer. Jesus' answer implies that he provides ultimate security ("eternal life") in another way, as shepherd of the flock the Father leads to him. And the rest of the Fourth Gospel helps us understand that one gains access to eternal life by accepting Jesus as sent by the Father and by laying down one's life for one's friends.

It is the episode from Acts, however, that best illustrates the earthly action prompted by Easter faith. Paul and Barnabas have been evangelizing their fellow Jews in a synagogue in Antioch of Pisidia. Meeting rejection from some of their coreligionists, they turn to the Gentiles. They justify this move with a telling use of Scripture: "So the Lord has commanded us, *I have made you a light to the Gentiles, that you may be an instrument of salvation to the ends of the earth*" (cf. Isa 49:6).

Notice that here Paul and Barnabas apply to themselves the very passage from Isaiah that Luke applies to Jesus in the Presentation account: Simeon alludes to this part of Isaiah when he holds the baby Jesus and refers to him as "a light for revelation to the Gentiles" (Luke 2:31). In today's reading from Acts we learn just how it is that Jesus becomes a light to the nations: as risen Lord working through his evangelizing disciples. Paul will take up this theme again when he explains to Herod Agrippa that the Messiah had to suffer and "as the first to rise from the dead, he would proclaim light both to our people and to the Gentiles" (Acts 26:23).

Easter would make evangelizers of us all.

Fifth Sunday of Easter

Readings: Acts 14:21b-27; Rev 21:1-5a; John 13:31-33a, 34-35

"I heard a loud voice from the throne saying, 'Behold, God's dwelling is with the human race.'" (Rev 21:3)

GOD WITH US

This Sunday's reading from Acts seems at first to offer little for meditation or celebration. Luke seems simply to be rounding off his account of the first mission of Paul and Barnabas. Having told about their preaching (to "mixed reviews") in Antioch of Pisidia, their roaring success among the pagans of Lystra, and the persecution by some of their unconvinced Jewish peers, Luke ends with a quick summary, retracing their route through seven towns and bringing them full circle to their home-base community in Syrian Antioch. But even this crisp summary, because of how it is told, carries food for the spirit.

Even in the midst of persecution, Paul and Barnabas make plenty of new disciples. Indeed, persecution becomes an engine of the mission. Resistance and harassment in one town leads them to receptive hearers in another. And when they retrace their steps to encourage recent converts, typically small communities in hostile environments, they preach, "It is necessary for us to undergo many hardships to enter the kingdom of God." This is precisely the wisdom Paul explores, on a more personal level, in his writings to the Corinthians (see 2 Cor 12).

Churches need leaders, and so "they appointed elders for them in each church, and with prayer and fasting, commended them to the Lord in whom they had put their faith" (14:23). No time for extended seminary training here. It is all so brisk, it looks like the hasty action of harried administrators, but the very phrasing lets us know that it was something else entirely. The appointments were done with prayer and fasting—that is, with a powerful physical and spiritual investment on the part of all. And this appointment of elders is carried out with a profound sense of collaboration with the risen Christ; they entrust these leaders to the Lord in whom they (the leaders) had put their trust (i.e., in their original Christian conversion).

When they come home to the community of Syrian Antioch, Luke can describe the place as "where they had been commended to the grace of God for the work they had now accomplished." This reminds us that Paul and Barnabas were commissioned by that community in the same way that they themselves now commission elders to preside in their local communities (Acts 13:1-3, the commissioning of Paul and Barnabas after much prayer and fasting).

As an indication of how they saw evangelization as a collaboration with God, Luke says, "When they arrived, they called the church together and reported what God had done with them and how he had opened the door of faith to the Gentiles" (14:27). Thus the ministry of evangelization is a matter of cooperating with something God is doing through the risen Lord. Christian mission enables people to discover God-with-them as they come to believe in the presence of Jesus risen. Luke describes it that way because that experience of the early Church is understood as a paradigm for what the Church continues to be and do. Luke is careful to insist that mission is a matter both of getting doors slammed in your face and of finding doors mysteriously opened. Easter teaches that, in the midst of much slamming, God is the great Opener.

Revelation 21 ponders that same divine presence with an image from Ezekiel 37:27. Seeing the new Jerusalem descending, John hears a loud voice from the throne saying, "Behold, God's dwelling is with the human race. He will dwell with them and they will be his people and God himself will always be with them." This, of course, is a vision of final union with God, but we can recognize that the post-Easter communities had already begun to speak of their communal life as being the very dwelling place or temple of God (see 1 Cor 3:16; 1 Pet 2:4-6).

The reading from John's account of the Last Supper takes us to the heart of what is going on in the Christian mission flowing from Easter. Instead of focusing on the offering of body and blood in the form of bread and wine (which this Gospel has already treated in connection with the feeding of the five thousand, in chapter 6), the Fourth Evangelist dwells rather on the profound action of the Master's washing of his disciples' feet. That action of service, Jesus says, shows them how they are to treat one another (John 13:14). That provides the background for "the new commandment" expressed in this Sunday's Gospel, which is also the deepest form of evangelization: "This is how all will know that you are my disciples, if you have love for one another." People observing a Christian community are supposed to be impressed that their kind of mutual service and love can only be explained by a divine presence they claim to know.

Sixth Sunday of Easter

Readings: Acts 15:1-2, 22-29; Rev 21:10-14, 22-23; John 14:23-29

> **"It is the decision of the Holy Spirit and of us not to place on you any burden beyond these necessities. . . ." (Acts 15:28)**

SPIRIT-LED DECISION-MAKING

Anyone who has written the minutes of a committee meeting knows that an account of the resolution of a major conflict will probably take more than a page or two. It is a sign of Luke's genius that he manages to catch the essential dynamics of the early Church's resolution of its first major crisis in twenty-nine lines.

Since the Lectionary edition of Luke's account of the "Council of Jerusalem" gives us only ten of Luke's twenty-nine verses, it will help to review the whole story. Imagine that you are a member of the Jerusalem community of Jewish Christians. You have accepted Jesus of Nazareth as the long-awaited Anointed One (Messiah) of Israel and, of course, you continue to think of yourself as a Jew and to meet in synagogue and to worship, when you can, in the Temple. Quite naturally, you assume that any Gentile who joins your "Jews-for-Jesus" group will follow the usual practice of proselytes. The Gentile will take on the practices of Torah, including, for males, circumcision. When you learn that Saul of Tarsus, up in Antioch, is allowing Gentiles to join the Jesus group without taking up such Jewish practices, you are understandably concerned. You are naturally inclined to agree with the Jerusalem leaders who say to the Antiochene Gentile converts, "Unless you are circumcised according to the Mosaic practice, you cannot be saved."

This, in a nutshell, is the first major crisis of the early Church. It requires a conference of the leadership. Most scholars agree that the resolution of this crisis was a lengthy process that surely required more than a single, brief meeting. Luke's account of the Church's resolution of this question, however, is not a matter of minutes for archives; it is an account meant to serve as a paradigm of ecclesial decision-making.

Note the dynamics of the process Luke outlines. First, the leaders acknowledge that they have a problem for which no extant policy offers a clear solution; so they decide to deal with this as a community by calling a meeting of the leadership ("apostles and presbyters"). Next, they review their experience. Peter rehearses his experience of being drawn into the Gentile mission through the remarkable conversion of Cornelius and his household. Then Paul and Barnabas describe "the signs and wonders God had worked among the Gentiles through them" (v. 12).

The assembly then interprets their experience of God working through them by looking to the longer experience of the community embodied in its Scriptures. This is exemplified by James' citing a passage from the prophet Amos (9:11-12; the Greek version), which implies two stages in God's plan for Israel: (1) the restoration of the people of Israel ("rebuild the fallen hut of David") and (2) the ingathering of the Gentiles ("so that the rest of humanity may seek out the Lord, even all the Gentiles").

The upshot: the Jerusalem council determines that mission to the Gentiles is the will of God, and that they ought to do all in their power to cooperate with this divine initiative. They decide, then, on a policy that both honors the tradition and adjusts to changing circumstances; they ask of Gentile converts only that they keep the minimal "rules for resident aliens" indicated in Leviticus (regarding marriages to relatives, food associated with idolatry, and improper slaughtering).

Finally, they boldly speak of this very human process (reflection on experience and interpretation in the light of tradition) as "the decision of the Holy Spirit and of us." If we wonder at their confidence, we can find its source reflected in this Sunday's Gospel reading, in which Jesus promises the presence of the Holy Spirit as an Advocate who will teach and remind the community after the departure of Jesus' physical presence.

These readings remind us that our Easter faith entails the remarkable belief that the Spirit of God continues to work through the very human processes of decision-making in our Church. Luke's paradigm urges us to take seriously both our religious experience and our tradition, and to trust that the Spirit of God works even (especially?) through endless debate, exhausting meetings, and hesitant leadership.

The feast of the Ascension, later this week, will further illustrate this reality, when Luke shows the apostles, gaping at the heavens, addressed with the words, "Men of Galilee, why are you standing there looking at the sky?" Easter, Pentecost, and Ascension thrust us forward into the mission of the Spirit-led Church.

Seventh Sunday of Easter

Readings: Acts 7:55-60; Rev 22:12-14, 16-17, 20; John 17:20-26

> **"I pray not only for them, but also for those who will
> believe in me through their word, so that they may
> all be one, as you, Father, are in me and I in you, that
> they also may be in us, that the world may believe
> that you sent me." (John 17:20-21)**

UNITY—AN OPTION?

The final words of the high priestly prayer of Jesus in John 17 contain a vision of Church whose message is so startling that, frankly, it stops me cold whenever I read it: the unity of the Church is to be such that, simply by example, it will convert the world. That is what the words say—twice, in case we didn't get it the first time (17:20-21, and again in vv. 22-23).

Those climactic words of Jesus' prayer in John's version of the Last Supper convey an unmistakable assertion about the mission of Jesus' followers: rooted in their participation in the union of Father and Son—facilitated by the Holy Spirit, we know from the earlier parts of the Last Supper discourse—they are to be so united that they convince nonbelievers that the group's claims about Jesus (as the revelation of the creator of the universe) must be true.

Has this ever happened? Can it possibly be a realistic hope? Yes, we can find in history times and places where the life of a Christian community has been such that its example of mutual service and love has drawn outsiders to join their number. As to whether it is a realistic hope, how can we deny that words expressed as a prayer of Jesus can be anything other than a divine mandate? What is mandated must lie within the reach of hope.

From the fuller context of the Fourth Gospel, especially the scene in which this prayer is set, we learn that the unity of Christians is to find its source and expression in the kind of mutual service that Jesus modeled in his washing of the disciples' feet. This action reflects precisely the core of Jesus' teaching on discipleship as we find it in the Synoptic Gospels—in Mark 10:44-45, for example: "Whoever wishes to be first among you will be the slave of all. For the Son of Man did not come to be served but to serve and to give his life as a ransom for many."

Ironically, just when the theologians of separated Christian denominations are arriving at new areas of consensus, those same denominations, and even local churches, are experiencing new internal divisions. It is a sobering sign of the times when a dying cardinal's call to his fellow U.S. Catholics for establishing a common ground in dialogue is met with suspicion and resistance. It was, remember, not a call to compromise in matters of doctrine and morality; it was a plea for a deeper level of discourse (speaking and listening) as we labor to move beyond suspicion and culture clashes in order to live out together what is essential in our common faith.

Luke's portrayal of the death of Stephen may hint at one of the resources for drawing unity out of conflict, even out of murder. One of the seven chosen by the Jerusalem Christian community to assist the apostolic Twelve, Stephen, at odds with the Synagogue of the Freedman, soon finds himself the victim of a rigged trial (complete with false witnesses) before the Sanhedrin. After he speaks his piece about how Jesus fits the pattern of God's plan (like Joseph and Moses, Jesus is a rejected leader who becomes his people's savior), Stephen has a trinitarian vision: "filled with the holy Spirit, he looked up intently to heaven and saw the glory of God and Jesus standing at the right hand of God" (Acts 7:55). He claims his vision is an assertion of the Son of Man as risen Lord.

When his adversaries move into an impromptu "lynching" by stoning, Luke describes Stephen's behavior in ways that precisely parallel the death of Jesus. (1) Like Jesus, he is taken out of the city to be dispatched. (2) Just as Jesus prayed to the Father, so Stephen prays to the risen Jesus, "Lord Jesus, receive my spirit" (this parallel is as clear a claim to the divinity of Jesus as is to be found anywhere in Acts). (3) Finally, like his Master, he cries out in a loud voice, "Lord, do not hold this sin against them."

What does the martyrdom of Stephen have to do with Jesus' prayer for unity? Just as Jesus' own death and resurrection release the power of the Holy Spirit to form a community for mission, so Stephen's faithful union with Father, Son, and Spirit works, even through his death by murder, to plant a seed in a bystander, Saul of Tarsus. This Pharisee, aiding the killers by minding their cloaks, will soon respond to a vision of the same Lord, and become the greatest promoter of Christian community we have ever known. Christian unity in our own day will come only through mutual service and forgiveness enlivened by that same trinitarian prayer.

Pentecost Sunday

Readings: Acts 2:1-11; 1 Cor 12:3b-7, 12-13; John 20:19-23

"To each is given a manifestation of the Spirit for the common good." (1 Cor 12:7; NRSV)

HAVE YOU SENT YOUR PENTECOST CARDS?

Most folks send Christmas cards. A few send Easter cards. Somewhere, someone may send out cards to celebrate Pentecost, but I haven't heard about it. And yet, I submit, it may help us think about the importance of this feast if we consider possible reasons—apart from boosting the greeting card industry—for celebrating the occasion by designing and sending Pentecost cards.

Pentecost is more than the afterglow of Easter; it is Easter's culmination. The Jewish feast of Passover (commemorating the release from captivity) finds fulfillment in the feast of Weeks (*pentecostēs* in Greek), commemorating the Sinai covenant. Similarly, Easter, celebrating the divine victory over the shame of death by crucifixion, finds its fuller meaning in the enlivening of the Christian community through the gift of the Holy Spirit. The thrust of Luke's history of the early Church in Acts is to illustrate how the risen Lord works through the community through its empowerment by the Holy Spirit. Weak Peter becomes a forceful leader. Incredulous disciples move from dejection into mission. The signs and wonders worked in Jesus' ministry by the power of the spirit now continue in the ministry of the "People of the Way." Peter, addressing the Jerusalem authorities in Acts 11, can speak of Pentecost as the time "when we came to believe in the Lord Jesus" (11:17), because until they had received the gift of the Spirit, they were not able to recognize just how it was that the risen Jesus was their Lord. Finally, empowered for their prophetic mission, they came to full faith in Jesus' lordship over their lives. Doesn't this warrant a card?

We believe in a Church. Just as we rightly single out the wonders of the incarnation (Christmas) and the redemption (the Easter Triduum) for special celebration, ought we not to celebrate Pentecost as the birthday of the Church? For we do boldly assert, in the Nicene Creed, that we believe in one, holy, catholic, and apostolic Church. That includes the remarkable conviction that the Spirit of the risen Lord directs and energizes a worldwide community of some two billion people baptized in the name of Jesus—half of us united with a pope and another half with whom we share an alliance wounded by past errors and agonies. While Christmas and Easter could leave us meditating in solitude at the crib scene or lost in wonder at the entrance of the empty tomb, Pentecost can awaken us to the startling communal dimension of our faith. We believe that the incarnate and risen Lord continues to work with this immense, sinful, gifted community to heal a wounded world. Doesn't this deserve at least a card?

Pentecost is about God-given unity in God-given diversity. When St. Paul wrote that first letter to the Christians in Corinth, he was addressing a group turned on to the spiritual gifts but divided by a variety of factions and rivalries. Some were boasting that the catechist who brought them into the faith was more authoritative than the teachers of others. Some were maintaining that their ability to speak in tongues indicated their superiority over others. Paul took the occasion of this division to teach clearly that any spiritual gift—healing, tongues, wisdom, leadership—was given not for the promotion of self but for the service and building up of the community.

To illustrate this insight, he developed his famous image of the body of Christ. Like the organs of a living body, the gifts of individuals derive their meaning not from their inherent excellence but from their contribution to the life of the body. What the Corinthians liked to call *pneumatika* ("spiritual things") Paul preferred to call *charismata* ("gifts"). If there was ever a time when the church was suffering from the challenge of working out our diversity of gifts rooted in the unity of the one Lord it is now. This is another reason to celebrate Pentecost as the feast that shows us the source and purpose of our diversity of gifts. In Paul's language, every Christian is charismatic and Spirit-filled.

The marketplace may not be ready for the Pentecost card. But thinking about Pentecost in connection with those other card-linked feasts, Christmas and Easter, may help us recognize the pride of place this commemoration deserves in our calendar of celebrations. It is about God working with us. It points to life in the Church now, as we respond to the news of incarnation and redemption by using our diverse gifts for the service of the one body of Christ.

Holy Trinity

Readings: Prov 8:22-31; Rom 5:1-5; John 16:12-15

> **". . . the love of God has been poured out into our hearts
> through the Holy Spirit that has been given to us."**
> **(Rom 5:5)**

From Experience to Doctrine

A rabbi I know is frequently asked to speak about Judaism to classes in Catholic schools. She marvels at the students' assumptions about Jewish understandings of God. "If you don't believe in the divinity of Christ," they sometimes ask her, "what does that do to your understanding of the Trinity?" That Jews have no concept of God as Trinity amazes the students; and their amazement continues to amaze the rabbi.

This reciprocal puzzlement can serve as a reminder that the Christian doctrine of the Holy Trinity is not a matter of reasoning, nor even a matter of revelation to be found in the Hebrew Bible. Our sense of God as triune is a doctrine that came from reflecting on God's revelation in the life, death, and resurrection of Jesus, who is called Christ and Lord only by Christians. Claiming a divine Christ raised the challenge of integrating that claim with the oneness of the God of Israel.

If it is the Christian experience of Jesus that gave rise to the teaching on the Trinity, then the only way even to begin to understand the doctrine is to reflect on the experience that prompted it. This Sunday's reading from Romans provides a fine entrance into such reflection.

The cutting from Romans 5 gives us a privileged glimpse into the heart of St. Paul's understanding of Christian life and faith. Paul writes to the Roman Christians for several purposes. He wants, for example, to demonstrate his way of teaching the faith and to help ease tensions arising naturally from the fact that the Christian community of Rome is comprised of people from two diverse and sometimes mutually hostile backgrounds—Gentile and Jewish. Up to this point in the letter, he has argued that all of them—Jew and Gentile alike—needed the gift of God that came in Christ Jesus; and, Jew and Gentile alike, they had all come into that new relationship with the Creator through the kind of faith modeled by Abraham, who trusted that God could bring life out of sterility.

At the point of today's reading, Paul begins a four-chapter section in which he rehearses some of his favorite ways of describing the transformation they have all experienced as baptized and believing Christians. He describes this, for instance, as moving from sinful solidarity with Adam to life-giving solidarity with the new Adam, Christ, or as moving from death to a new life, or as like being adopted slaves who gain a new family and an astounding inheritance as children of God.

Here, in Romans 5:1-5, Paul gives his résumé of the Christian experience, which he knows the Roman Christians have shared even though he has not met them yet. Without fear of being presumptuous or misunderstood, Paul can assert that he and his readers are people who have peace with God. When we read "peace" in Paul we should think *shalom,* which means not simply the absence of strife or guilt but the fullness of shared covenant life in relationship with the Creator. Paul uses language from his Jewish heritage to describe what he has come to see as the fulfillment of that heritage. He adds that this new realization of life with God has been enabled by "our Lord Jesus Christ." That is the creed in a nutshell: Paul knows that, with the Roman Christians, he claims the Galilean Jesus of Nazareth is the long-awaited Messiah of his people, and, leaping beyond his past Jewish expectations, this Jesus is worthy of the divine title "Lord."

He writes, "through whom we have gained access by faith to this grace in which we stand, and we boast in hope of the glory of God." This *shalom* in Christ Jesus has a future. The death and resurrection of Jesus founds a hope of sharing in the very glory of God. Meanwhile, this relationship sustains us in the midst of the hard stuff of life: "we even boast of our afflictions, knowing that affliction produces endurance, and endurance proven character, and proven character hope, and hope does not disappoint, because the love of God has been poured out into our hearts through the holy Spirit that has been given to us." "Love of God" here is not our love of God but God's love of us.

There we have it—the seeds of the later full-blown doctrine of the Trinity rooted in experience. Like the cross, the sense of God as Trinity is "scandal to Jews and folly to Gentiles." But for those who believe in Jesus as Messiah and Lord, the doctrine of God as three Persons is not mainly an intellectual puzzle but a necessary description of the experience of those who are enabled by faith to pray through the Son to the Father in the Holy Spirit.

The Body and Blood of Christ

Readings: Gen 14:18-20; 1 Cor 11:23-26; Luke 9:11b-17

> **"For as often as you eat this bread and drink the cup,**
> **you proclaim the death of the Lord until he comes!"**
> **(1 Cor 11:26)**

PAUL ON THE LORD'S SUPPER

You wouldn't know it from this Sunday's excerpt from 1 Corinthians, but Paul is hopping mad when he writes this community about their way of celebrating the Lord's Supper in that town. As it happens, the words cited comprise the earliest account of the Last Supper. But Paul rehearses this institution narrative, as it is called, not out of archival interest but to make a powerful point in his critique of the Corinthian Christians' treatment of one another. The fuller context, 1 Corinthians 11:17-34, is crucial to our understanding of Paul's intent in recalling what happened "on the night [Jesus] was handed over."

Several facts regarding the social setting need to be taken into account. First, we need to remember that at the time Paul writes, there were as yet no buildings specifically constructed for Christian worship. Christians gathered in the homes of people wealthy enough to have sufficient room for such a gathering (places like Philemon's in Colossae, for example). Second, the scene implied in Paul's letter implies the early Christian practice of combining the Lord's Supper with a normal meal.

And third, archaeologists tell us that the dining area of a larger Roman home—and Corinth was, at this time, a Roman colony—included a *triclinium,* which was, as the word suggests, a three-sided chamber in which the more privileged guests (typically, nine) could recline around a low table; then there was a larger area, the *atrium,* where other, less important, guests could gather to eat. In other words, as in our airplanes today, there were first-class guests and then there were second-class guests, with the quality of the service and the menu graded accordingly.

The scene Paul addresses fits such a set-up exactly. He notes that in their "coming together" they do not really come together at all. For the more privileged and wealthier among them eat heartily and get drunk, whereas the poorer members get less, and some are even left out. The social gap between rich and poor becomes evident in their celebration of the Lord's Supper.

It is precisely to confront this scandal of division where there should be unity that Paul recites the tradition that he had already passed on to them when he had originally catechized them. The rehearsal of the solemn account of the Last Supper is meant to shock them into the realization that their failure to care for one another's needs in their practice of the Lord's Supper flies in the face of the very meaning of that ritual enactment. The Lord's Supper—what we have come to call the Eucharist (from Greek) or the Mass (from Latin)—commemorates Jesus' "handing over" of himself for our redemption; thus our celebration of that event should be evident in our "handing over" of ourselves to one another, at least in seeing that each is decently fed.

Paul drives this point home a few lines later, when he says, "For anyone who eats and drinks *without discerning the body*, eats and drinks judgment on himself" (11:29, emphasis added). The fuller context of his passage (especially 10:17, "because the loaf of bread is one, we, though many, are one body, for we all partake of the one loaf") makes it clear that by "discerning the body" Paul means seeing the believing community as the one body of Christ. And so, however the rest of their culture may discriminate between privileged and nonprivileged guests at dinner gatherings, Christians, when they come together for the Lord's Supper, are to "receive" one another as mutual guests. The kind of equality expressed in Paul's motto quoted in Galatians 3:28 ("neither Jew nor Greek, neither slave nor free person, . . . not male and female . . .") is to be evident especially at the Lord's Supper.

Paul's intent, then, in quoting the tradition of the Last Supper, is not to develop a eucharistic theology but to remind them of the loving behavior entailed in the meaning of the Lord's Supper. Retrieving Paul's context offers a powerful reminder to us that our eucharistic celebrations commit us to truly behave as the one body we have become through baptism into the body of Christ.

The Nativity of St. John the Baptist, June 24

Readings: Isa 49:1-6; Acts 13:22-26; Luke 1:56-66, 80

> **"John heralded his coming by proclaiming a baptism of repentance to all the people of Israel." (Acts 13:24)**

THE BAPTIST AND US

What does it mean for the Christian community to celebrate the birth of John the Baptist as one of the twelve date-linked solemnities in our liturgical calendar? Though the Church rightly calls him "saint," John was not a Christian. He was not around for Easter and Pentecost, the events that made it possible to be baptized into the body of Christ. His own water ritual was a baptism for repentance, a prophetic symbolic action facilitating his call for recommitment among his fellow Israelites. How then are we to celebrate him as part of our Sunday Eucharist? As always, the readings chosen for the feast are our best help for focusing our prayer and worship.

The passage from Isaiah 49 is one of the famous Servant Songs, those four oracles that portray Israel's role in Yahweh's saving action among the nations. In the language of the songs, the Servant sometimes stands for the covenant people as a whole, and sometimes Servant means an individual embodying and leading Israel. Both senses are present in the second song, today's reading from Isaiah. We hear the Servant of Yahweh reflecting on his vocation. He had at first thought that his vocation was simply to gather together the scattered tribes of Israel (awesome enough); now, he says, the Lord God has an even greater mission: "I will make you a light to the nations."

The writers of the New Testament, Luke especially, saw this promise fulfilled especially in Jesus and the Church. But the passage is fittingly read to celebrate the Baptist, because he was a special agent in that first stage, the restoration of Israel. That was the purpose of John's revival campaign, calling Israel to renewed dedication. In this he plays the role of the Servant of Yahweh in an explicit way.

The second reading, from Peter's speech to the synagogue in Antioch of Pisidia, speaks of the Baptist heralding Jesus' coming by proclaiming a baptism of repentance "to all the people of Israel." This is mentioned as an essential part of the way that "God, according to his promise, has brought to Israel a savior, Jesus." Part of John's preparation for Jesus' Servant ministry was the training of some of the men who were to become Jesus' first disciples.

Finally, the Gospel furthers our appreciation of John's role in the history of salvation. The extended family of Elizabeth and Zechariah are gathered from what is, after all, a celebration of the Abrahamic covenant, which looked forward to Israel's becoming a "blessing for the nations" (cf. Gen 12:1-3). Even the word used by Jews today for circumcision—*brit* (from *berith*, "covenant")—reminds us that this rite is about entering the covenant community. That makes the ritual a renewal of something old and enduring.

That there is also something profoundly new about to occur in the life and mission of John is signaled by the fact that this new life springs from a woman who had been sterile. The promise of that new life had so stretched the faith of Zechariah that he had at first doubted it could happen. That incomplete response expressed itself physically in the loss of his speech (and apparently hearing) until his obedient insistence that the child be named John restored his speech.

Space requires that our Lectionary omits the canticle that issues from that freed tongue (the Benedictus), but our celebration of John should include some meditation on those words. For they describe his role powerfully: "And you, child, will be called prophet of the Most High, / for you will go before the Lord to prepare his ways, to give his people knowledge of salvation / through the forgiveness of their sins, because of the tender mercy of our God, / by which the daybreak from on high will visit us / to shine on those who sit in darkness and death's shadow, / to guide our feet into the path of peace" (1:76-79).

We celebrate John the Baptist with solemnity because his faithful work as prophet of the covenant was so central to the way God chose to bring salvation to us in Jesus. His role as prophet of Israel helps us understand that the new covenant in Jesus was a renewal, not a replacement, of God's *brit* with Israel. We Gentile Christians are the beneficiaries of John's fidelity to that covenant.

Eighth Sunday of the Year

Readings: Sir 27:4-7; 1 Cor 15:54-58; Luke 6:39-45

"From the fullness of the heart the mouth speaks." (Luke 6:45)

TALKING THE WALK

There is a cluster of traditional sayings underscoring the insight that the character of a person shows itself most truly in deeds more than in words. "Talk is cheap," we say, meaning that what a person actually does is far more important than the promises that person makes. "She doesn't just talk the talk; she walks the walk," we say, meaning that the woman lives out what she professes. These sentiments are particularly strong during political campaigns.

This is true enough, and there are plenty of biblical passages to show that the insight is perennial. But the first and last of this Sunday's readings focus on another aspect of our "talk life"—the utter importance and power of our words. Talk may well be cheap in the case of an empty promise or sly flattery. But both Jesus ben Sirach and Jesus bar Joseph give us words today that remind us that some of our most significant deeds are in fact the words we say.

For better or worse, our speech reveals who and what we are. Sirach demonstrates this in three sharp images. The act of speech is like sifting wheat through a sieve: as the sifting sorts out the husks, so our speech exposes the otherwise hidden faults of our character. And just as the hot fire of a kiln tests the craft of the potter, so the give and take of conversation tests the integrity of the interlocutors. Finally, just as the quality of a fruit tree indicates the care of its cultivator, so our speech reveals everything that has gone into our formation.

One could meditate on that imagery and draw the fatalistic conclusion, "Well, you are what you are, and your speech is going to show it no matter what you try to do about it. Maybe it's best to keep quiet."

Jesus of Nazareth, mediated today by the evangelist Luke, puts the reality of our speech in a fuller context. "A good person out of the store of goodness in his heart produces good, but an evil person out of the store of evil produces evil; for from the fullness of the heart the mouth speaks" (6:45). By itself, that teaching seems to leave us with Sirach: for better or worse, your speech is going to show you up. But Jesus' words come attached to the rest of the Sermon on the Plain (Luke 6:20-49).

Jesus' sermon presents a bracing challenge to our "talk life." Jesus addresses his teaching "to you who hear," meaning those poor enough to be responsive to his words. He then proceeds to urge love of enemies, nonviolence, selfless giving, and a compassion that imitates God's own mercy. The heart that the mouth reveals is supposed to be that kind of heart! That might sound more discouraging than Sirach, except that Jesus' teaching on prayer throughout the rest of the Gospel of Luke reminds us that the power to imitate Jesus in these matters is not our own. It comes from the gift of the Spirit given in prayer, which in turn enables us to become those who listen to Jesus' words and act on them.

When we put all this in the larger setting of the story of Jesus and the story of the Church in Acts, we recognize that full discipleship is not only a matter of walking the talk; it also entails "talking the walk." That is, some of the most important Christian deeds will in fact be acts of speech, challenging injustice, encouraging the downhearted, asking and giving forgiveness, blessing with praise those who need to be affirmed.

Paul reminds us that the heart that produces the goodness revealed in speech is the heart that is rooted in the risen Lord Jesus. "[Know] that in the Lord your labor is not in vain" (1 Cor 15:58).

Ninth Sunday of the Year

Readings: 1 Kgs 8:41-43; Gal 1:1-2, 6-4; Luke 7:1-10

"For I too am a person subject to authority . . ."
(Luke 7:8)

WE GENTILES

Most of us Catholics—at least those born before 1950—grew up with the presumption that Jesus came to start a new religion and that the New Testament somehow rendered the Old Testament irrelevant. In the period since Vatican II, a careful rereading of history has helped us realize that Jesus was undeniably Jewish (as indeed were all of the earliest Christians) and that most of us contemporary Christians are Gentile heirs of the faith of Israel, albeit reshaped around the person and teachings of Jesus. This Sunday's readings can help us appreciate some of the connections.

In the selection from 1 Kings, the author we have come to know as the Deuteronomist shows Solomon making a public prayer at the dedication of the first Temple. Earlier in this prayer, Solomon had reflected on this construction as the fulfillment of God's promise to David through the prophet Nathan, that not David but David's son (Solomon) would build a house for God and that, meanwhile, God would build a "house" (dynasty) for David. Further, Solomon reflects on the paradox of building a dwelling place for God, who in fact is not even contained by the highest heavens (still, human beings need a place in which to honor the transcendent God). And in the part chosen as today's reading, the king prays for the Gentiles he envisions coming to the Temple to honor the God they have come to know through Israel's experience of Yahweh. This picks up on the divine promise to Abraham that "all the communities of the earth" would find blessing in him (Gen 12:3).

It is precisely such a foreigner that we meet in today's Gospel. Remarkably, an administrator of the hated Roman occupation, a centurion stationed in Peter's adopted town, Capernaum, has become a friend and benefactor of the very people whose land his militia occupies. "He loves our nation and built the synagogue for us," the town elders tell Jesus. Such benefaction is not simply tolerance; it is involvement in Israel's worship, for synagogues were thought of as distant extensions of the Jerusalem Temple's precincts. These village multipurpose meeting places of study, prayer, and adjudication were architecturally oriented to the Temple in Jerusalem. He is exactly the kind of Gentile envisioned in Solomon's prayer. He has come to know Israel's God through the people. And now he recognizes in Jesus the manifestation of that God.

Even in his approach to Jesus, the centurion is careful to acknowledge the Israelite community of faith. He does not send some of his soldiers to summon Jesus. Rather, he asks the local Jewish elders to mediate for him. He even refrains from insisting on a "house call" from Jesus and insists that a simple command on Jesus' part will suffice for the healing of his servant.

We should take seriously the interesting parallel the centurion draws when he explains his reason for trusting so deeply in Jesus' power to heal: "For I too am a person subject to authority, with soldiers subject to me. And I say to one, 'Go,' and he goes; and to another, 'Come here,' and he comes; and to my slave, 'Do this,' and he does it" (7:8). He perceives that Jesus' power to heal comes from his being under the authority of the God of Israel and therefore mediates the divine power that comes with that authority.

That parallel may strike contemporary ears as a misplaced metaphor, but we should take it seriously. Only two chapters earlier, Luke, in his account of the healing of the paralytic, says, "the power of the Lord was with him for healing" (5:17). In his humanity, Jesus acts in the manner of a prophet. The Son acts in the authority of the Father. The Gentile centurion has come to recognize this, and in this he becomes an heir of the faith of Israel in the God who works through mediators.

It is telling that Luke places the account of the healing of the centurion's servant immediately after the Sermon on the Plain (Luke 6:22-49). We Gentile readers of Jesus' teaching to assembled Israel are, like the good centurion, invited to share in Israel's faith in a God who sends healing mediators, most especially that Jewish mediator for all humanity, Jesus.

Tenth Sunday of the Year

Readings: 1 Kgs 17:17-24; Gal 1:11-19; Luke 7:11-17

> **"Fear seized them all, and they glorified God,
> exclaiming, 'A great prophet has risen in our midst,'
> and 'God has visited his people.'" (Luke 7:16)**

A PROPHET, AND MORE THAN A PROPHET

A man perceived by his peers as a prophet revives the only son of a widow. That summary describes both the first and the third of this Sunday's readings. The Gospel accounts of Jesus' healing (and resuscitation) ministry parallel no part of the Hebrew Bible more than the stories of the signs and wonders wrought by the prophets Elijah and Elisha. When the editors of our Lectionary pair Elijah's restoration of the widow's son with Jesus' resuscitation of the son of the widow of Nain, they are simply reflecting Luke's own awareness of the parallel. Luke provides a hint of this awareness when he explicitly echoes a phrase from 1 Kings 17. The Deuteronomist (the scholars' name for the author of the books of Kings) writes, "Taking the child, Elijah brought him down into the house from the upper room and *gave him to his mother*." Compare Luke's phrasing: "The dead man sat up and began to speak, and Jesus *gave him to his mother*." A closer look at the two accounts can help us appreciate both the similarities and the differences.

First, the similarities. Both Elijah and Jesus take the initiative: Elijah says, "Give me your son," and Jesus tells the widow not to weep and stops the funeral procession by touching the coffin. In both cases a dying or dead son is restored to his mother, and people respond by acknowledging this restoration as an act of God.

But noting these similarities only serves to highlight the differences. Whereas the son in 1 Kings is clearly dying (he has stopped breathing), the son of the widow of Nain is declared dead by Luke as he is being carried to his grave. In each case the involvement of the prophet is notably different: whereas Elijah carries the dying boy to his guestroom bed, lies down on top of him, and prays to God for the return of the life breath, Jesus simply addresses the corpse, "Young man, I tell you, arise!"

The difference in the nature of the respective prophet's authority is underscored by the use of the name "Lord": whereas Elijah prays to the Lord God, Luke refers to Jesus himself as "the Lord" ("when *the Lord* saw her, he was moved with pity for her . . ." [7:13]). And the language of the response to the wonder is more open-ended and suggestive in the case of Jesus: whereas the widow simply sees the restoration as the authentication of Elijah as a prophet ("now indeed I know that you are a man of God"), the stunned members of the funeral procession at Nain say that much and more: "A great prophet has arisen in our midst," and "God has visited his people." Although, from the perspective of the speakers these statements are synonymous, in the perspective of Luke that second acclamation at Nain recalls that Jesus the prophet is more than a prophet; he is Son of the Most High and conceived by the Holy Spirit (Luke 1:31-35). God has indeed visited his people more intimately than they suspected at that moment in the village of Nain.

And why would Luke want us to reflect on these parallels and differences? His account of the resuscitation at Nain brings home some powerful realities. The healing ministry reveals the same compassionate God experienced by the people of Israel who celebrated the divine action in the prophets Elijah and Elisha. But Jesus is a "visitation of God" even more profoundly and completely than that experienced in those earlier prophets. At the same time, that divine manifestation was fully incarnate in the person and career of a true prophet of Israel. Jesus, a prophet and more than a prophet, now risen Lord of the Church, still shows himself in the healing of minds and bodies when we open ourselves to his presence in faith, prayer, and action.

Eleventh Sunday of the Year

Readings: 2 Sam 12:7-10, 13; Gal 2:16, 19-21; Luke 7:36–8:3

"'The LORD on his part has forgiven your sin.'"
(2 Sam 12:13)

THE FORGIVEN LIFE

The first and third readings for this Sunday both deal with forgiveness, and both are linked to parables. The prophet Nathan's confrontation with David follows right after a famous parable, one of the few in the Hebrew Bible (2 Sam 12:1-7). To help the king acknowledge the heinousness of his murder of Uriah (in order to possess Bathsheba), Nathan plays a parabolic trick on him. "Judge this case for me," he says. He then proceeds to tell the story of a rich man who takes and kills a poor man's pet ewe lamb to serve up to a visitor. When David responds to this account in rage ("As the LORD lives, the man who has done this merits death!"), Nathan confronts him with the reality hidden behind what was really a parable masked as a legal case: "You are the man!" For the arrogant injustice of the rich man is only a pale image of David's lust-driven act of murder. The "case" that turns out to be a parable about David is only the first surprise. There is a second: Nathan informs the king, "The LORD, on his part has forgiven your sin."

Like the prophet Nathan, Jesus, in today's Gospel, uses a parable to open arrogant eyes. And, as in the case of David, divine forgiveness appears in a surprising way. The Pharisee who hosts Jesus sees a woman, reputed to be a sinner (the nature of her sin remains undisclosed), who enters the dining area and proceeds to wash Jesus' feet with her tears, dry them with her hair, and then kiss them and anoint them with perfumed oil. That Jesus allows such a woman to touch him (and so sensually) disqualifies him as a prophet in the eyes of the Pharisee. Knowing the Pharisee's thoughts, Jesus does what Nathan did with David, proposes a situation for the Pharisee's judgment: A money lender forgives two debtors, one owing 50 coins, the other 500. Which would be the more grateful? The one forgiven more, of course. Then Jesus describes how the woman's startling actions really made up what had been lacking in the Pharisee's hospitality. Whereas the Pharisee had been distantly relating to Jesus only to size him up and to find reason to reject him and his message, she had fully responded to Jesus' call to repentance.

"So I tell, you," Jesus says, "her many sins have been forgiven because she has shown great love. But the one to whom little is forgiven, loves little."

But wait a minute. Was not the point of the parable that loving gratitude is a *response* to having been forgiven? Now Jesus' words to the Pharisee seem to say that the loving behavior somehow preceded (and merited?) the forgiveness. This apparent contradiction points to a translation problem often noted by commentators. The wording of the Greek original of Luke 7:47 is ambiguous. A literal rendering would be "her many sins have been forgiven, seeing that she has loved much"—leaving unresolved whether the love is the *occasion* (cause) or the *evidence* (effect) of the forgiveness. The translators of the 1986 version of the New American Bible translated the verse, "So I tell you, her many sins have been forgiven; hence, she has shown great love," explaining in a note, "That the woman's sins have been forgiven is attested by the great love she shows toward Jesus," insisting that "this is also the meaning demanded by the parable in verses 41-43." That the current Lectionary editors have chosen to stay with the more traditional rendering of the verse should not distract us from the essential biblical teaching that God's forgiving love precedes and invites our grateful repentance.

That theme of the priority of God's loving action comes through powerfully in Paul's words in the reading from Galatians: "Insofar as I now live in the flesh, I live by faith in the Son of God who has loved me and given himself up for me" (Gal 2:20). The faith that saves is a grateful response to God's loving and forgiving initiative. It can even lead to exuberant tears, the washing of feet, and kissing.

Twelfth Sunday of the Year

Readings: Zech 12:10-11, 13:1; Gal 3:26-29; Luke 9:18-24

> **"Whoever wishes to be my follower
> must deny his very self, take up his cross each day,
> and follow in my steps." (Luke 9:23)**

CARRYING YOUR CROSS

The saying quoted above, about carrying one's Cross, is one of those that the Jesus Seminar dismisses as not plausible on the lips of the historical Jesus. Surely, they say, the reference to the cross is meaningful only after the crucifixion; thus, they surmise, it must be the creation of the post-Easter Church.

A little imagination, however, suggests that this is not necessarily the case. Death by crucifixion had long been an established fact of life in the Near East. It was the Roman mode of capital punishment for noncitizens guilty of serious crimes—runaway slaves, for instance. The vertical beam on the mound called Skull Place at the western gate of Jerusalem stood as a constant reminder of this harsh sanction. The condemned ("dead men walking") could be seen, from time to time, carrying the crossbeam on the way to the place of execution.

The point of making the convict carry the crossbeam was not so much to induce physical discomfort as to mark him for public shaming. It was the empire's way of saying, "Here is a public enemy! Insult freely and spit at will!" Given that common experience, Jesus' saying to his disciples during his pre-Easter ministry makes perfectly good sense: "Following me will likely entail your getting shamed. The way of life to which I call you is not embraced by the world at large. Following me will inevitably mean rejection." Does this not make perfectly good sense coming from the historical Jesus?

Obviously, the metaphor of carrying the cross took on a more profound meaning after Jesus quite literally did it and then was raised from the dead. But considering how it would have been heard before Easter helps us get in touch with its post-Easter meaning.

Over the centuries, Christians have extended the idea of carrying one's Cross to any and all suffering that comes along, and it is true that any suffering accepted in the right spirit (from a burdensome relative to a terminal illness) can be redemptive. But when the New Testament speaks of Christian suffering, it is almost always a reference to *apostolic* suffering—suffering incurred in the course of carrying out one's Christian mission. Recalling the probable setting of Jesus' image (the shaming of the convict) helps us retrieve what was likely the original focus— that is, not some spooky extra dose of physical suffering but a side-effect of living out one's discipleship with courage.

Thirteenth Sunday of the Year

Readings: 1 Kgs 19:16b, 19-21; Gal 5:1, 13-18; Luke 9:51-62

[Jesus] answered him, "Let the dead bury their dead. But you, go and proclaim the kingdom of God." (Luke 9:60)

Jesus—Gentle and Demanding

I once heard a Samaritan scholar give a talk at the Omaha Jewish Community Center. At one point he said, "We Samaritans and you Jews are both heirs of the ancient Israelite tradition. We Samaritans carry the authentic tradition, whereas you who have lived to the south of us are the heretics. The Torah says nothing about a temple in Jerusalem. Deuteronomy speaks about worshiping in 'the place where I will cause my name to dwell.' We know where that is—Shechem and Mt. Gerizim." To my surprise, the audience received this statement quite calmly. The quarrel was, after all, twenty-six centuries old. They knew what to expect when they had invited a Samaritan to speak to them.

It is precisely this ancient quarrel that Luke expects his readers to know about when he writes that the Samaritans would not welcome him "because the destination of his journey was Jerusalem." To Samaritans, a group of Jewish Galileans on their way to worship in Jerusalem was a group of heretics acting out their heresy; the Galileans were crossing Samaritan turf for the wrong reason and therefore deserved not hospitality but contempt. Confronted by this hostility, James and John (the "Sons of Thunder"), inspired perhaps by Elijah's ability to summon divine pyrotechnics (1 Kings 18 and 2 Kings 1), ask, "Lord, do you want us to call down fire from heaven to consume them?" Luke says simply that Jesus turned toward them only to reprimand them and that they set off for another town.

Surprisingly, this passage is little used as a demonstration of Jesus' teaching and practice of nonviolence. Yet it is one of the best examples of his teaching on nonretaliation. He knows where the Samaritans are coming from. Rather than return hate for hate, he understands, forgives, and moves on.

Then, after this stunning example of tolerance, there follows an episode demonstrating how profoundly demanding Jesus can be. When Jesus summons a potential disciple, the man makes what appears to be a reasonable request: "Let me go first and bury my father." Jesus replies, "Let the dead bury their dead. But you, go and proclaim the kingdom of God."

Jesus' reply would be stark indeed if it were a refusal to allow the son to attend to his recently deceased father's funeral and burial. But the situation may be quite other than what we assume. In first-century Palestine, it was customary that the eldest son stay home, manage the property of his aging parents, and finally see to their proper burial. If that is the situation implied here, Jesus' reply is not a command to skip a parent's funeral. Rather it is a challenge to leave home *now*—not some thirty years hence—to join in the Master's mission. Urgent and challenging, yes; cold and unreasonable, no.

With a little background, these puzzling episodes at the start of Jesus' journey to Jerusalem become powerful illustrations of the cost of discipleship, anywhere and any time. Jesus still invites all of us, not just mendicants and celibates, to break free from the expectations of our culture when the mission of announcing and enacting the reign of God demands it. More frequently than we may like to admit, that commission invites us to respond to misunderstanding and hostility with compassion and nonviolence.

Fourteenth Sunday of the Year

Readings: Isa 66:10-14c; Gal 6:14-18; Luke 10:1-12, 17-20

"[Wear] no sandals; and greet no one along the way."
(Luke 10:4)

TRAVEL TIPS

It is all very well to read Jesus' commissioning of the disciples with its curious restrictions (no walking sticks, no backpacks, no sandals, no greetings on the way). But what does that have to do with following Jesus today?

We are familiar with Jesus' commissioning of the Twelve in Matthew, Mark, and Luke; only Luke, however, gives the account of the sending of a further group of seventy (or seventy-two, depending on which manuscript you read). Where does this extra group come from? It may indeed be literally a further group that Jesus sent out during his public ministry. Then again, this account may be the Third Evangelist's way of previewing the mission of the post-Easter Church reaching out to the nations. For 70 is the classic biblical number of the nations of the world, as illustrated by the "Table of Nations" in Genesis 10. (The alternate number of 72 in the manuscripts may well derive from the fact that the Greek version of Genesis 10 lists 72 nations.) And so, this commissioning of the 70/72 may well intend to say something about the Church's mission generally, not just the mission during Jesus' time. Given the fact that the Christian communities portrayed in Acts and reflected in the letters of Paul were mainly made up of urban stay-at-homes, Luke probably wants us to use this picture of the sending of the 70/72 as a kind of symbolic paradigm for the living of the Christian mission generally. Taken this way, what can it mean?

The harvest is abundant but the laborers are few; so ask the master of the harvest to send out laborers for his harvest. Imaging the mission as a harvest reminds us that the enterprise is one initiated by God, not simply a human project. In spreading the Good News, we participate in something God is doing. Conscious contact with the Harvest-master, i.e., prayer, is essential.

Do not carry a walking staff or traveling bag; wear no sandals. No one in their right mind traveled the Palestinian roads staffless, bagless, and unshod. Without a staff you are defenseless. Without a bag of some kind, you have no way of carrying a change of clothes or some bread for the road. And no matter how tough your feet are, you can't run from danger on that rocky terrain without something on your feet. In short, anyone traveling in this strange way would be engaged in a kind of prophetic action, communicating by means of attention-getting behavior. The point of this mode of traveling would seem to be something like this: we are people who trust in God for our defense and who depend on the hospitality of others for our sustenance; we have a vision to share.

Greet no one along the way. In the Near Eastern setting, the point here is not avoiding the courtesy of giving or responding to a friendly greeting; it is rather a mandate not to engage in the extended pleasantries and exchanges that were customary in those parts. The point of this travel style is not unfriendliness but moving with an air of urgency.

How does this apply to Christians (then and now) who live in town and hold down a steady job? The missionary charge to the 72 suggests that even followers of Jesus who are registered voters with a permanent address should be people who "travel light," live a little more trustingly than the culture around them, and exhibit a sense of purpose that clearly goes beyond producing and consuming goods and getting entertained. Even settled Christians can live in a way that invites questions about where such people are coming from and where they think they are going.

Fifteenth Sunday of the Year

Readings: Deut 30:10-14; Col 1:15-20; Luke 10:25-37

But because he wished to justify himself, he said to Jesus, "And who is my neighbor?" Jesus replied: "A man fell victim to robbers as he went down from Jerusalem to Jericho." (Luke 10:29-30)

WHO IS YOUR SAMARITAN?

To Jesus' fellow Jews, a Samaritan was a despicable creature. We tend to miss that important fact. Because we have monumentalized the hero of Jesus' road-rescue story by naming hospitals and laws after the Good Samaritan, we have lost touch with the fact that the relationships between first-century Jews and Samaritans were generally characterized by that special hostility found among close relatives who feel themselves betrayed by the other. Missing that note, we also miss much of the punch of the parable.

Luke had already alluded to that animosity in chapter 9 when he wrote that the Samaritans "would not receive him" as Jesus and his disciples headed south through Samaritan territory to Jerusalem. Any Samaritan knew that the proper place for authentic Israelite worship was Mount Gerizim and that Galilean Jews on pilgrimage to Jerusalem were heretics busy doing the wrong thing—people out of place. A parallel with our experience of gangs and "turf" is not out of place here.

In his typical way, Luke provides a specific occasion for the telling of the parable. A teacher of Torah, bent on testing Jesus, asks the Big Question: "What must I do to inherit eternal life?" Jesus questions the questioner by asking what the teacher reads in his Torah. The lawyer responds with a nice summary of Jesus' own Torah-linked teaching, joining love of God (Deuteronomy 6) with love of neighbor (Lev 19:18). Embarrassed that Jesus has exposed him as knowing the answer to his own question, the teacher, in true forensic fashion, asks Jesus to define "neighbor." The implication is that once you define "neighbor," you know the designated "neighborhood," and then you also know whom you can hate, or at least neglect.

Instead of responding with the requested definition, Jesus tells a story with details carefully chosen. A man is assaulted and robbed in a setting that would have been familiar and plausible to first-century Palestinians. The road from Jerusalem to Jericho—desolate and full of twists and turns—is still a likely place for highway robbery. Stripped and unconscious, the victim becomes a kind of "common denominator" of humanity. Without the cues of clothing and speech, there is no way to place him by race or class; it is not even clear whether he is living or dead.

When we hear about those who pass by without helping the victim, we easily dismiss them as heartless religious officials. The response of Jesus' original audience may well have been more nuanced. The victim—naked, motionless, and mute—would look to the casual glance like a corpse. Among the purity regulations that constrained the lives of Temple officials (priests and Levites) was a rule saying that touching (even coming within four cubits of) a corpse rendered one unclean. The narrative, then, allows us to understand the by-passers' behavior as "playing it safe" in the presence of what seemed to be a corpse rather than cold neglect of a robbery victim. The original listeners would not have been surprised.

By contrast, the action of the Samaritan traveler is astounding. This man has every excuse in the world to mind his own business and to keep on moving. A Samaritan in Judea, on the wrong "turf," he is himself an automatic target for hostility. If he is caught near the victim, he would be considered a likely suspect in the aggression. Yet he is "moved with compassion at the sight" and proceeds to place himself at risk by administering first aid and taking the victim to an inn to see that he is properly cared for.

In answer to the lawyer's quest for a self-serving definition of neighbor, Jesus has provided this stunning narrative image, as if to say, "You ask for an exclusive definition of 'neighbor'; I say: *Be neighbor* to any human being in need."

At a time when our tribal hostilities tear at national and even ecclesial unity, this parable of Jesus challenges us to take our membership in the human family with utmost seriousness.

Sixteenth Sunday of the Year

Readings: Gen 18:1-10a; Col 1:24-28; Luke 10:38-42

> **"Lord, do you not care that my sister has left me by**
> **myself to do the serving? Tell her to help me."**
> **(Luke 10:40)**

MARTHA UNMASKED

This Sunday offers two famous biblical scenes of hospitality—Abraham receiving the three travelers, and Martha and Mary hosting Jesus.

In Genesis 18, Abraham, following the conventions of good Bedouin courtesy, scrambles to receive some passing travelers. The scene turns out to be a theophany, a revelation of God. The narrator introduces the three passers-by as "three men." Eventually, one of the three turns out to have extraordinary powers, for he predicts that Abraham's wife will bear a son next year. A few verses on in this chapter (vv. 13 and 14), the author confirms what the reader (and Abraham?) suspects, namely that this mysterious member of the trio is none other than "the Lord" (Yahweh). In this account, it is not Abraham's hospitality that is the focus; it is rather the Lord's surprising fulfillment of the covenantal promises (see Genesis 12, 15, and 17), bringing fertility to the sterile bodies of Abraham and Sarah. This account has inspired the famous Russian icon interpreting Abraham's visitors as the Trinity.

In Luke's scene of hospitality, the primary guest is again called "the Lord"—this time, the Lord Jesus. But here the focus is on the behavior of the hosts. Like Abraham, Martha is busy about many things—no doubt preparing the food. Mary simply sits at Jesus' feet, listening to his words. Martha complains to Jesus that she is left with all the work and says, regarding the contemplative Mary, "Tell her to help me." Jesus chides Martha and defends Mary.

Christian tradition has applied this passage in discussions of the relative worth of active and contemplative lifestyles in the community of faith. Jesus' language about "need of only one thing" and "the better part" do lend themselves to that application. But the placement of the Samaritan parable right before should be enough to tell us that Luke does not understand this account to champion contemplation as superior to action. The point of Jesus' critique of Martha lies not in her activity but in her self-preoccupied comparison. In this case, the one thing necessary was attending to the guest—whether by cooking or by attentive conversation. Martha's fault was to be distracted from the point of her activity—serving the guest. The New Testament frequently images Christian life as hospitality. Whether we are Martha or Mary is beside the point, if we focus on serving the guests.

Seventeenth Sunday of the Year

Readings: Gen 18:20-32; Col 2:12-14; Luke 11:1-13

**"See how I am presuming to speak to my Lord, though
I am but dust and ashes!" (Gen 18:27)**

ASK AND YOU SHALL RECEIVE

Jesus' parable about the friend who begs bread from his neighbor at midnight, is it really about persistence? Or is it about something else? To think fresh thoughts about this story, it helps to know five bits of background information. First, in the Ancient Near East, it was taken for granted that one offered a meal to a visiting traveler. Second, bread (think pita) was essential to any meal in that culture; grain in the form of bread was a major part of the diet and it also served as a utensil (you broke off pieces to dip into common serving bowls). Third, since baking occurred out of doors, in an oven shared by several families, everyone knew who baked bread on a given day. Fourth, the reputation of a village for hospitality was a matter of community honor. And fifth, there is a fascinating question regarding the proper translation of the word commonly rendered as "persistence."

Note that this brief similitude (the kind of parable that makes a comparison with a common occurrence in daily life) comes in the form of a complex question which can be rendered this way: "Which of you who has a friend will go to him at midnight and say to him 'Friend, lend me three loaves, for a friend of mine who is on a journey has just come to me and I have nothing to put before him,' and he from within will answer, 'Do not disturb me; the door is now closed, and my children are with me in bed; I cannot get up and supply you'?" The implied answer to that question is, "None of us would receive such a response; even the grouchiest of neighbors would help out in a situation like that."

Indeed, Jesus' next comment confirms this interpretation. For he says, "I tell you, if he does not get up to give the visitor the loaves because of their friendship, he will get up to give him whatever he needs because of his [*anaideia*]." Before we translate the word left in Greek, ask yourself if it is a quality of the would-be host or of the sleepy neighbor. Does the *anaideia* not belong to the sleeper? And what does it mean? The root *aideia* means shame; and the *an-* prefix is the negative indicator, what they call the alpha-privative. This has led some scholars to conclude that the sentence should be translated something like this, "He will get up and give him whatever he needs because of his avoidance-of-shame." And that does indeed spell out what was implied in the situation sketched in Jesus' question. *Even if the guy next door is a grouch, you know he will come through with the bread to avoid dishonoring the village's reputation for hospitality.*

On this interpretation, the point of the parable is not persistence but assurance. And this is precisely the point made in the sayings that follow (vv. 9-13), e.g., "Ask and you will receive. . . . If you then, who are wicked, know how to give good gifts to your children, how much more will the Father in heaven give the Holy Spirit to those who ask him?" There are other parables that do teach persistence in prayer, notably The Importunate Widow (Luke 18:1-8). But everything in the context of Luke 11 points to the assurance that the Father to whom we pray "Give us each day our daily bread" will indeed do so. What's more, he will even give us the ultimate Gift, the Holy Spirit.

In an age when some would denigrate prayer of petition as somehow symptomatic of immaturity, we do well to recall Jesus' basic teaching on prayer: even grown-ups are supposed to deal with God like a hungry child asking a parent for food, or a neighbor requesting a necessity.

Eighteenth Sunday of the Year

Readings: Eccl 1:2; 2:21-23; Col 3:1-5, 9-11; Luke 12:13-21

**"Thus it will be for all who store up treasure for
themselves but are not rich in what matters to God."
(Luke 12:21)**

HOARD, AND YOU SHALL LOSE

It is hard to miss the point of the parable of the Rich Fool: you can't
take it with you. But that is a bit of ancient wisdom, hardly requiring
Christian revelation. It is an obvious human truth already clearly
stated in Ecclesiastes: "Here is one who has labored with wisdom and
knowledge and skill, and yet to another who has not labored over it,
he must leave property." The Lukan parable goes deeper than the bald
facts of human mortality and the transiency of material possessions. A
careful reading of the story shows it to be a brilliant cartoon illustrat-
ing how greed destroys all the covenant relationships. Let's read it
slowly, following the more literal rendering of the New Revised Standard Version.

The land of a rich man produced abundantly. Notice that the subject of
the sentence is the land. This reflects the Jewish insight that, whatever
may be the human contribution in the process of farming, it is the land,
the earth, that is the source of food. Thus an abundant crop, like the
land itself, is a gift of God. The Sabbath no-work law is meant to help
people stay in touch with this reality. It will become clear that the land
owner of the parable has lost touch with this dimension of his relationship with the Creator.

*And he thought to himself, "What should I do, for I have no place to store
my crops?"* The very phrasing of the question shows the consequences
of forgetting that land and crops are divine gifts: the man has also lost
the sense of stewardship that flows from that perception; he has forgotten the Torah wisdom that the goods of the earth are meant to meet

the needs of all, not simply the desires of those who happen to manage the land. This landowner speaks too easily of "my crops." For him, the unexpected abundance is not a boon for the community; rather it presents a crisis of personal assets management.

Then he said, "I will do this: I will pull down my barns and build larger ones, and there I will store all my grain and my goods. And I will say to my soul [psychē], *'Soul* [psychē], *you have ample goods laid up for many years: relax, eat, drink, be merry.'"* No mention of the larger community here; it is a question of "my grain and my goods." The fact that this man is pursuing an interior monologue in a vacuum of selfishness is conveyed by the humorous sound of, "I will say to my soul, 'Soul . . .'"— or, in a translation that catches the humor ever better, "I will say to myself, 'Self. . . .'"

But God said to him, "You fool! This very night your life [psychē] *is being demanded of you. And the things you have prepared, whose will they be?"* Surprise, surprise—a forgotten auditor is heard from: the Creator. There is an economic image here, suggesting the translation: "This night they will foreclose on this 'self' of yours . . ." Even one's self is a gift.

Thus the man stands revealed as having allowed his greed to destroy all his covenant relationships—with the earth, with his community, with himself, and with God. Is it possible that this neglected parable has something to say to us?

Nineteenth Sunday of the Year

Readings: Wis 18:6-9; Heb 11:1-2, 8-19; Luke 12:32-48

**Faith is the realization of what is hoped for and
evidence of things not seen. (Heb 11:1, NAB, 1986)**

WAITING FOR WHAT?

In his dramatic report of a 1996 ascent of Mount Everest, *Into Thin
Air,* Jon Krakauer describes the risks, discomfort, and expense that
some people are willing to endure in order to reach their goal, reaching
"the rooftop of the world," the mountain's summit at 29,028 feet.

Viktor Frankl, in his account of what he learned about human nature
in a Nazi concentration camp, *Man's Search for Meaning,* notes that the
people most likely to survive that ordeal were those who had something to look forward to—a loved one with whom they hoped one day
to be reunited or an enterprise they hoped to accomplish.

What we look forward to is so deeply a part of our personality that
this mental and spiritual reality impacts on our bodily health and vi-
tality. The lack of something to look forward to results in a deteriora-
tion of energy and performance, and in its extremity can lead to suicide.
Recalling this helps us understand the importance of the elements of
Christian faith that theology calls eschatology ("the last things")—
death, judgment, heaven, hell.

In some times and places, preaching and teaching was so preoccupied with the last things that religion thus practiced was labeled by
Marxists as "the opium of the people." Their point: the more people focused on the afterlife ("pie in the sky by and by"), the less they were inclined to attend to the injustices of the way things are now. Political
oppressors were all in favor of such otherworldly religion.

In response to such misplaced investment in the next life, the Church
has rightly reminded itself (recently, in Vatican II) of the importance of
taking seriously the gifts and tasks of our earthly life, short though that

sojourn may be. Now, many of us, having absorbed that lesson—the importance of our present daily lives—need to become reawakened to the forward-looking dimension of our faith. This Sunday's readings can help us do just that.

The passage from the book of Wisdom features the Israelites beside the Red Sea, the pharaoh's charioteers on the horizon, waiting confidently for the divine rescue to come. They knew their faith was not in vain because Yahweh's ten signs and wonders had already facilitated their exodus out of slavery.

Chapter eleven of the letter to the Hebrews displays the famous "cloud of witnesses"—Abraham chief among them—showing how trust in God founded on past experience of God (in Abraham and Sarah's case the experience of life drawn from sterility) enables the faithful to move into an unknown, and even improbable, future.

The Gospel's parables of the servants and the returning master encourage a balance regarding attention to future reward (or punishment) and to present responsibilities. The first story highlights the unpredictability of the future moment of judgment ("be on guard, therefore"). The second parable underscores the importance of right behavior in the present; the servants are given responsibilities (dispensing the ration of grain in season). The steward who is found doing that upon the master's return is rewarded. The one who abuses his authority by taking advantage of his situation is punished. The wisdom of these parables is caught in the Last Judgment scene that dominates the decor of medieval cathedrals. Attention to that image awakens the worshiper to a future reality; but that future fact of judgment calls one right back to the realities and responsibilities of this life—the deeds we do now that will be mercifully and justly evaluated in the future.

Twentieth Sunday of the Year

Readings: Jer 38:4-6, 8-10; Heb 12:1-4; Luke 12:49-53

**Let us . . . persevere in running the race that lies
before us while keeping our eyes fixed on Jesus, the
leader and perfecter of faith. (Heb 12:1-2)**

JESUS, PERFECTER OF FAITH

How can the Prince of Peace, the preacher of the message of nonviolence that we hear in the Sermon on the Mount—how can he speak the
hard words of today's Gospel? "Do you think that I have come to es-
tablish peace on the earth? No, I tell you, but rather division." Then
Jesus proceeds to promise the most painful kinds of division—within
households, even between parents and children. Can these sayings be
reconciled? They can, when we recognize that those words of division
do not describe Jesus' mission but rather some of the side-effects of
that mission.

That his mission should have divisive results should not surprise us.
Recall the prediction of Simeon at the Presentation: "Behold, this child
is destined for the fall and rise of many in Israel, and to be a sign that
will be contradicted . . ." (Luke 2:34). And such indeed was the effect
of Jesus' public life—from the rejection at the synagogue of Nazareth
to the divided response of the bandits crucified on either side of him.

The creation of the new family of the Church would continue to pro-
voke as much rejection as acceptance—even to the splitting of households and families. But even as today's readings confront us with this
hard picture of prophetic mission constantly rejected—from Jeremiah,
through Jesus, down to us—the bit from the letter to the Hebrews is
there to console us.

Here, the author of Hebrews presents Jesus himself as a model for
the Christian persevering through tough challenges "for the sake of
the joy that lay before him." He dares to call Jesus the "perfecter of

faith"—in other words the one whose *own* faith showed what true faith is. This phrase is so startling that some translations (e.g., KJV, NIV, NRSV, NAB [1970]) add the possessive pronoun "our" (apparently to avoid imputing faith to Jesus). But other versions—notably the Rheims, the New American Standard, and the NAB (1986)—stay close to the Greek and support the meaning demanded by the context, namely that it really is Jesus' own trust in the Father that we are called to imitate. That faith sustains us through any and all rejection.

Twenty-First Sunday of the Year

Readings: Isa 66:18-21; Heb 12:5-7, 11-13; Luke 13:22-30

"When once the master of the house has risen to lock the door and you stand outside knocking and saying, 'Sir, open for us,' he will say in reply, 'I do not know where you come from.'" (Luke 13:25)

INSIDERS AND OUTSIDERS

All we know of heaven and hell comes to us in the form of images drawn from our ordinary human experience. Apart from Dante's imaginings, my candidate for the most powerful scenario of hell is the one in this Sunday's Gospel, quoted in part above. You arrive at a banquet to which you thought you were invited—and find yourself rejected at the door by the host. The image of eternal fire is frightening enough, but permanent rejection from the place where you thought you belonged— this, it seems to me, is an even more daunting prospect.

The image of the reign of God as banquet was central to Jesus' preaching and mission. He drew it from Isaiah, it seems, and made it his own. "On this mountain," says Isaiah, "the LORD of hosts / will provide for all peoples / A feast of rich food and choice wines, / juicy, rich food and pure, choice wines . . . / He will destroy death forever" (25:6-8). This is a picture of God's salvation—a *shalom* that is universal ("all nations"), centered among the chosen people ("this mountain"—i.e., Zion), and ultimate ("he will destroy death forever"). But, as always in these celebrations of God's final victory, the Good News is accompanied by bad news for those who resist God's reign: "For the hand of the LORD will rest on this mountain, / but Moab will be trodden down / as a straw is trodden down in the mire" (v. 10).

This Sunday's reading from the last chapter of Isaiah draws upon another expression of that image of a final and universal gathering at end-time Zion. In this context, the nurturing is expressed not in the image of a banquet but in the more intimate one of a mother nursing a child at her breast. Again, the reach is fully inclusive: the nations accompany the scattered children of Israel home, and some of the Gentiles even get to serve as Temple priests. But the larger context of the passage also includes a sorting out: whereas "all mankind shall come to worship" Yahweh, yet the saved "shall go out and see the corpses of the men who rebelled against me" (Isa 66:23-24).

Jesus took that banquet-gathering image a step further. He illustrated—or, better, demonstrated—his proclamation of God's reign in his action, his hosting of meals to which even tax collectors were invited. When religious officials challenged this behavior, Jesus defended this practice by telling the parables of the Lost Sheep, the Lost Coin, and the Two Lost Sons (Luke 15, where the prodigal son's return is celebrated in a banquet from which the elder son absents himself). As in Isaiah, the reach of the banquet is universal, but the response of those invited results in a sorting out of happy insiders and excluded outsiders. Jesus spells this out in the parable of the Great Feast (Luke 14), where those first invited absent themselves with vapid excuses and the feast is shared with the wretched brought in from the highways and byways.

Today's Gospel stresses the lot of those who have become outsiders through their failure to respond to the invitation. Exclusion does not come from lack in the "wideness of God's mercy." People are flocking in from north, south, east, and west. Those standing outside are in fact presumptuous evildoers.

This stark image of Jesus is a wake-up call. The Good News of the kingdom carries warning that we could "blow it," permanently, if we refuse the gift and task of the Gospel.

Twenty-Second Sunday of the Year

Readings: Sir 3:17-18, 20, 28-29; Heb 12:18-19, 22-24a;
Luke 14:1, 7-14

> **"Rather, when you are invited, go and take the lowest**
> **place so that when the host comes to you he may say,**
> **'My friend, move up to a higher position.'" (Luke 14:10)**

WHO IS YOUR PATRON?

If the previous Sunday's Gospel focused on Jesus' use of Isaiah's banquet image for the end-time gathering, this Sunday's Gospel shows Jesus using that festal metaphor to illustrate "kingdom behavior" in the banquet of our present life.

In a culture that made much of places of honor at a banquet, Jesus advises guests to take the lowest place, to get the host to honor you by calling you to a higher place. Notice that he is not challenging the system of places of honor. He does not even seem to be challenging the *desire* for a place of honor. Apparently he is simply supplying a clever strategy for gaining that higher place.

You will find commentators who claim that Jesus is not speaking parabolically here but is literally giving a kind of seating-for-success advice for scoring honor points at banquets. Such an interpretation hardly squares with Jesus' teaching elsewhere (e.g., in the parable of the Pharisee and the tax collector) that the disciple really is supposed to humble himself or herself.

Taking the teaching as straight advice, however, does serve to point up an apparent contradiction: in speaking of humbling oneself, Jesus still seems to keep exaltation as the goal. In other words, humble behavior is advised as a means to honor. Is he saying this? Well, yes. But notice that Jesus is shifting the location of the honor. He is acknowledging that any human being wants honor, but he is challenging people to acknowledge that the patron whose good opinion really counts in their lives is God. That is the meaning of the saying, "Whoever exalts him/herself [before other people] will by humbled [i.e., by God] and whoever humbles him/herself will be exalted [by God]." It is not a matter of groveling or social manipulation; it is a matter of seeking approval from the Patron whose opinion really counts.

In this teaching, Jesus echoes the first reading, from Sirach: "My child, conduct your affairs with humility, / and you will be loved more than a giver of gifts." So far, it could be Ann Landers talking. But the next verse expands the horizon to a vision Jesus shares: "Humble yourself the more, the greater you are, / and you will find favor with God" (Sir 3:17-18).

Twenty-Third Sunday of the Year

Readings: Wis 9:13-18b; Phlm 9b-10, 12-17; Luke 14:25-33

> "Perhaps he was separated from you for a while for this
> reason: that you might possess him forever, no longer
> as a slave but as more than a slave, a beloved
> brother. . . ." (Phlm 15–16)

SOMEONE ELSE'S MAIL

We hear Paul's letter to Philemon so infrequently—it turns up in our
Sunday readings only once every three years—that it is worthwhile to
pause and savor it when it appears. Perhaps more than any other New
Testament document, this brief note (25 verses) helps us realize that
when we read an epistle of Paul we are reading someone else's mail. As
in the case of most personal correspondence, the sender presumes much
on the part of his receivers: e.g., knowledge of Paul's location (in prison,
but where?), Philemon's venue (Colossae? Col 4:9 refers to Onesimus as
"one of you"), the context of the slave's running away (sheer desire for
freedom? fear of reprisal for mismanagement on his part?). Much of
what the original readers/listeners knew we can only guess at.

Other things are clear. Philemon hosts a church gathering that meets
regularly at his house. Onesimus is Philemon's slave and he has run
away—a capital crime in the Roman Empire. Paul is sending him back,
expecting not only reconciliation but something "more" (manumis-
sion?). Though much of the letter has the sound of a personal note, it
turns out to be a very public document. Paul names Timothy along
with himself as a sender of the letter, and he mentions five other imprisoned fellow Christians who know he is sending this message. And
the addressees of the letter are not only the three named at the outset
but "the church that meets at your house" as well—a reminder that
first-century writings were typically intended to be performed orally
by a reader for a group.

It is hard to imagine Paul saying to fellow prisoners Luke and Mark, "You know, guys, this is such a fine letter, I'll bet that one day they'll make it part of the Bible." And yet, the letter to Philemon stands securely among the twenty-seven books of the New Testament canon. Why? Simply because St. Paul wrote it? But the New Testament is more than a reliquerium. Because Onesimus, freed for mission, eventually became the Onesimus mentioned as bishop of Ephesus fifty years later by Ignatius of Antioch? Possibly, but we don't know for sure.

The best reason for being enshrined in the canon may well be the letter's (implied) teaching about baptism, conversion, and Christian community. Notice the kinship language Paul uses throughout the note: Timothy is called "brother," Philemon is "beloved," Apphia is "our sister," Onesimus is "my child"—"fathered" by Paul during his imprisonment (because Paul has "parented" the slave into the new life of Christian faith). For Philemon, the consequence of Onesimus' conversion to Christ is that the runaway is no longer simply a slave but a "brother in the Lord."

In this family language we find a dramatic and concrete expression of the principle Paul alluded to in Galatians 3:28 ("There is neither Jew nor Greek . . . neither slave nor free person . . . not male and female; for you are all one in Christ Jesus"). Baptism into the body of Christ has created an equality of dignity that transcends distinctions grounded in race, law, and even gender. Rather than call for the abolition of the institution of slavery—a prospect beyond the wildest imagination of a member of a small movement in a huge and powerful empire—Paul nonetheless plants a seed that, with painful slowness, came to fruition centuries later.

This sensitive and clever letter of intercession illustrates well the point of this Sunday's Gospel. When Jesus lays down the shocking teaching that following him entails a readiness to turn one's back on family members, he is naming a stark consequence that accompanies good news: finding and following the will of God in Jesus makes us part of a new family that goes deeper (and wider) than blood. That was a stretch for Philemon and a risk for Onesimus. It remains so for us—which is why this letter, originally "someone else's mail," made it into the Bible.

Twenty-Fourth Sunday of the Year

Readings: Exod 32:7-11, 13-14; 1 Tim 1:12-17; Luke 15:1-32

> **"Tax collectors and sinners were all gathering around to hear Jesus, at which the Pharisees and the scribes murmured, 'This man welcomes sinners and eats with them.'" (Luke 15:1)**

PRODIGAL FATHER, TWO LOST SONS

The fact that Jesus "ate around" with people the authorities considered unclean clearly annoyed those officials. Indeed such behavior rendered Jesus suspect in their eyes. It was expected that a careful, Torah-keeping Jew did not share the table with those who did not eat according to the Law's prescriptions.

In defense of that behavior, Jesus tells parables. Luke lines up three here, each of them intentionally jarring. Jesus compares his table fellowship with the typical behavior of a shepherd seeking a lost sheep and a woman looking for a lost coin. In each case, the finding is cause for community celebration. Similarly, Jesus says, the return of repentant sinners is a matter of heavenly joy. Implication: Jesus' table fellowship is the occasion of welcoming the return of sinners, and the Pharisees and scribes refuse to recognize what is happening and to join the celebration of this manifestation of the kingdom of God.

But these two similitudes are simply the warm-up for the full-blown parable that follows, what might be titled "The Two Lost Sons." Here the tax collectors are represented by the runaway wastrel son, who realizes that his greediness has taken him away from his real source of life and security—his father—and he comes home to a surprising welcome. The Pharisees and scribes are portrayed as the stay-at-home elder son, who is also, in his own way, lost. He was able neither to confront the shameful initiative of his kid brother nor will he join his father's celebration of the runaway's return. The elder has failed to appreciate that his dad is a father, not a slave master (v. 30, translates literally, "all these years I *slaved for you* and never disobeyed one of your commands"). And the father, of course, symbolizes a compassionate God who forgives repentant sinners even as he challenges those who think they have no need to repent.

Twenty-Fifth Sunday of the Year

Readings: Amos 8:4-7; 1 Tim 2:1-8; Luke 16:1-13

> "I tell you, make friends for yourselves with dishonest
> wealth [the mammon of unrighteousness], so that
> when it fails, you will be welcomed into eternal
> dwellings. . . . You cannot serve both God
> and mammon." (Luke 16:9, 13)

THE PRICKLIEST PARABLE OF *ALL*

The parable long known as "The Unjust Steward" may be the most puzzling of all the stories of Jesus. Since it appears to present an immoral person as a model, the story has been used by Christianity's enemies to denigrate Jesus as teacher. But there is a way of reading it that makes powerful sense.

It is undeniable that the steward is called unrighteous and that he is also held up as some kind of an example. But just how is he unrighteous and exactly what aspect of his character or action is presented for imitation? Let's read it closely.

The steward of a wealthy landowner is told to turn in his books when he has been discovered as having squandered his master's property. No details are given regarding the nature of the mismanagement. Remarkably, the steward is not jailed, just "let go." Until he hands over the books, he still has authority over the land renters. He seizes this opportunity of his master's lenient dismissal (no debtor's jail) to curry favor with those renters. He moves quickly to "sweeten" their annual rent contracts (paid in kind according to their crop—i.e., in jars of olive oil or bushels of wheat). For example, he tells a farmer who cultivates olive trees that the rent this year will be cut by 50 percent. And a wheat grower will have to pay only 80 percent. They are instructed to alter the rates in their own hand because that is the usual way of formally acknowledging rental agreements. They do not know the steward is being dismissed; they would presume that he has talked the master into these more favorable

100

rates and would be only too happy to accede to the new contract, no questions asked. They would also think highly of the master for being so generous. When the landowner discovers what his steward has done, he has to hand it to him. The clever action of the steward has not only put the rascal in good favor with the renters; it has also brought to the landowner an honor which he would be foolish to try to undo.

Verse 8b suggests that the steward is some kind of example: "For the children of this world are more prudent in dealing with their own generation than are the children of light." Obviously, to imitate the steward literally, i.e., by acting deceptively, would simply be to act as a child of this world. Something else is required of the children of light. Jesus urges the latter, those trying to live the way of the kingdom, to "make friends for yourselves with dishonest wealth [the familiar "mammon of iniquity" in the Rheims and the KJV], so that, when it fails, you may be welcomed into eternal dwellings" (v. 9). Clearly this draws a parallel with the parable: Jesus urges us to use wealth in such a way as to gain favor with the One who is both the ultimate client and the ultimate landowner—God. Jesus spotlights the opportunistic shrewdness of the steward. The application for the "children of light" is that they too are to be clever opportunists, by using wealth in the ways that Jesus elsewhere advocates the use of resources—feeding the hungry, clothing the naked, lending but asking nothing in return.

The next four verses spell this out by way of a poem on mammon. "Mammon" is an Aramaic word meaning wealth or property. It is related to another Semitic word familiar to us—"amen." Root *mn* forms a verb meaning to trust in or believe. Thus property or wealth is called *mammon* because wealth is precisely what most people ("the children of this world") trust in for their security. If you are a child of light, you place your ultimate trust in God, not in mammon. Once we focus on that root sense of *mammon* ("the trusty stuff"), we can hear some meaningful wordplay in verses 11-14: "If, therefore, you are not trustworthy with ['the mammon of iniquity,'] who will trust you with true wealth? If you are not trustworthy with what belongs to another [i.e., the Ultimate Landowner], who will give you what is yours [a place in the 'eternal tents']? No servant can serve two masters . . . You cannot serve both God and mammon." This is precisely the basis of Jewish and Christian social ethics. The goods of the earth belong to God. Human beings are stewards of those resources to serve the needs of all.

Pull a dollar out of your billfold and prayerfully consider that we routinely print "IN GOD WE TRUST" on our mammon. Meditate on the question: "What in God's eyes would be my cleverest use of the wealth I steward?" Why is our Pope as critical of materialistic capitalism as he is of atheistic communism?

Twenty-Sixth Sunday of the Year

Readings: Amos 6:1a, 4-7; 1 Tim 6:11-16; Luke 16:19-31

"Woe to the complacent in Zion." (Amos 6:1)

DIVES AND LAZARUS

If the story of Dives and Lazarus, especially the request that the deceased Lazarus be sent to haunt the rich man's brothers, reminds you of Marley's ghost in Dickens' *A Christmas Carol,* you are right on target. Dickens himself admitted that this parable inspired his famous story. And there is much more in Jesus' parable to engage the imagination. While the main message of the story is clear enough, closer study reveals ironies that only serve to drive the message home more deeply.

First there is the matter of names. Ironically, the rich man goes nameless, whereas we are told at the outset that the beggar is called Lazarus. Tradition has tried to make up for this by calling the rich man *Dives,* which is simply the Latin word for "rich man." The irony is that while it is a preoccupation of the "great ones" of this world to be remembered, it is one of the "nameless ones"—the beggar, who gets named in the story. A further irony around names: after death, when "Dives" calls upon Abraham for a drink of water, he refers to Lazarus by name, indicating that he was very much aware of this man starving at his gate. Further, although Dives had not bothered to send a servant to meet Lazarus' needs, he has the arrogance to try to make an errand boy of Lazarus to quench his own thirst.

Then there is the matter of meals. The story really presents two meal scenes. The first scene is that of the rich man dining sumptuously, while Lazarus remains a conspicuous *non*-diner at his gate. The second scene, the afterlife of both individuals, shows Lazarus "in the bosom of" Abraham. The phrase "in the bosom of" refers to the position of honor at a banquet, the place where a favored guest reclines next to the host (see John 13:23); thus Lazarus is pictured enjoying first place at the heavenly

banquet, while the rich man is now clearly the one on the outside looking in. This image illustrates elements in Luke's version of the Beatitudes and "Woes": "Blessed are you who are now hungry, / for you
will be satisfied. . . . But woe to you who are filled now, for you will be
hungry" (6:21, 25). And Abraham's taunt ("My child, remember that
you received what was good during your lifetime while Lazarus like-
wise received what was bad; but now he is comforted here, whereas
you are tormented") plays on the wording of the first "woe": "But woe
to you who are rich, / for you have received your consolation" (6:24).

Abraham's words at the end supply the final irony: "If they will not
listen to Moses and the prophets, neither will they be persuaded if
someone should rise from the dead." Within the plot of the parable, the
statement refers of course to Dives' suggestion that Lazarus be sent to
spook his brothers into repentance. Within the larger context of the
Gospel, however, Abraham's words refer to the resurrection of Jesus
and the fact that the meaning of Jesus' life and teaching are in continu-
ity with the Law and the Prophets. And those who refused to respond
to the Law and the Prophets will fail to respond to the person and
teaching of the risen Lord.

All Dives needed to know was right there in the Hebrew Scriptures.
Indeed, a key passage in Isaiah addresses precisely his neglect of Lazarus: "This . . . is the fasting that I wish . . . / Sharing your bread with
the hungry, sheltering the oppressed and the homeless; / Clothing the
naked when you see them, / and not turning your back on your own"
(Isa 58:5-6). Lazarus was apparently homeless, surely hungry, and
even naked (dogs licked his sores). Jesus' moral teaching reaffirms the
covenant code outlined in the Torah and affirmed by the prophets.

We need not look further than this Sunday's first reading to find another example of prophetic warning to the rich. Amos satirizes the self-
indulgent wealthy who have become oblivious to the decline of their
society ("the collapse of Joseph"). The letter to Timothy adds its own
wake-up call: "I charge you to keep God's command without blame or
reproach until our Lord Jesus Christ shall appear." The final judgment
that comes with the parousia will test all by the light of the basic commands of the Torah—commands, that is, about acting according to the
covenant relationships, respecting life, speaking the truth, helping the
stranger, the widow, the orphan, the homeless, the hungry, the naked.

Twenty-Seventh Sunday of the Year

Readings: Hab 1:2-3; 2:2-4; 2 Tim 1:6-8, 13-14; Luke 17:5-10

> **"So you also, when you have done all that you were
> ordered to do, say, 'We are worthless slaves;
> we have done only what we ought to have done!'"
> (Luke 17:10, NRSV)**

Unprofitable Servants, Worthless Slaves?

Translate it how you will—"unprofitable servants" (KJV, Rheims, NAB [1986]), "useless servants" (NAB [1970]), "unworthy slaves" (NASB), "worthless slaves" (NRSV)—as a self-description of the Christian disciple, the phrase does not sound like good news to our North American ears. In a culture that reminds us from every TV monitor and most counseling offices that the point in life is to "feel good about yourself," who wants to cultivate the self-image of worthless slave? Yet there it sits—that phrase—as the punch-line in a parable whose context suggests that it is supposed to say something about faith.

If we are to hear the Good News in this parable, there are at least two barriers that we who live in the U.S. at the end of the twentieth century need to overcome: (1) our feelings about slavery and (2) determining the proper translation and meaning of that troubling adjective (rendered in the examples above as unprofitable, useless, worthless, unworthy).

About slaves we need to face several facts. First, the text really does say "slaves." *Douloi* is Greek for "slaves." Since most servants in the first-century Mediterranean world were slaves, "servants" is an *adequate* translation, but it loses some of the power of the metaphor. "Servants" bypasses the fact that, in that time and place, such slaves/servants were the *property,* not the *employees,* of their masters. Moreover, both Jesus and the early Christian writers were very much at home using slavery as a positive metaphor for one's relationship with God and even with the members of one's community. In those cultures, slavery was simply a fact of life, with some two-thirds of the population consisting either of slaves (frequently, people working off a debt) or former slaves. Jesus dared to teach that his followers were to be slaves of one another (e.g., Mark 10:44; same word, *doulos*). Paul was happy to identify himself as a "*doulos* of Christ Jesus" (e.g., Rom 1:1). And the earliest extant Christian hymn celebrates the humanity of Jesus as his taking on "the form of a slave [*doulos* again]" (Phil 2:7). Though it does not sell well in contemporary democratic culture, our ancestors were at home with the concept of subservience—to God and to one another.

Now, about the adjective describing the slaves in the punch-line of the parable—*achreioi*. Kenneth Bailey (to whose commentary I am indebted here) makes a good case that the word can be rendered "to whom nothing is owed." In other words, the point of the parable is that just as a household slave is not an employee of his master—i.e., never *earns* anything when he carries out his duties, so we, when we have lived out our covenant relationships with God and with one another, have simply done our duty and have "earned" nothing.

The good news in this image of our life with God is that, in living the life of faith, we come to see that we have a secure role in the "household of God"—an early metaphor for the community of the Church. Like a household slave, we belong in that household even more than an "employee" would. Though our own culture would not lead us to express all this in the imagery of slavery, properly understood, the parable expresses the same Gospel (Good News) truth that St. Paul communicates when he teaches in his letters that the Christian is saved by our faith. Paul's teaching on this relationship is powerfully summarized in Ephesians 2:8-10: "For by grace you have been saved through faith, and this is not from you; it is the gift of God: it is not from works, so no one may boast. For we are his handiwork, created in Christ Jesus for the good works that God has prepared in advance, that we should live in them." Even if Bailey is wrong, and the phrase is best rendered with something like "unprofitable servants" and "worthless slaves," once we get the point of seeing through the eyes of faith that our life is lived out in the honor and security of the "household of God," the good news comes home. Ironically, recognizing that we are unprofitable slaves in such a situation can help us "feel good about ourselves"—but for reasons very different than the ones preached by our time and place.

Twenty-Eighth Sunday of the Year

Readings: 2 Kgs 5:14-17; 2 Tim 2:8-13; Luke 17:11-19

> **"One of them, realizing that he had been cured, came
> back praising God in a loud voice. He threw himself
> on his face at the feet of Jesus and spoke his praises.
> This man was a Samaritan." (Luke 17:15-16)**

WHAT THE SAMARITAN SEES

When Naaman the Syrian is cured of his skin disease, he asks Elisha
permission to haul off a pile of dirt. What is the deal about the dirt?
This is a puzzlement for us twentieth-century readers because we do
not link the presence of God with geography. Things were different in
the world of the Ancient Near East that provides the context for Elisha's
healing of Naaman. In that time and place, every group had their
own, local god. It was a breakthrough for the Israelites to acknowledge that their god, Yahweh, was in fact not just the god of Israel; Yahweh was the creator of all and therefore God of all. Therefore, when
Naaman is healed in the name of the God of the Israelites, he comes to
the same insight: "Now I know that there is no God in all the earth,
except in Israel" (2 Kgs 5:15). But, since he has come to recognize that
the God of all is especially the God of Israel, he wants to honor that
fact by taking home as much of the land of Israel as he can pack into a
two-mule cart.

This interest in the proper place to find the presence of God carries
over into the Gospel account of Jesus' healing of the ten lepers. In
subtle ways (for the details, see Hamm, "What the Samaritan Leper
Sees: The Narrative Christology of Luke 17:11-19," *Catholic Biblical
Quarterly* 56.2 [1994] 273–87), Luke makes much of sacred geography
in this narrative.

Luke is careful to note that this episode occurs "along the borders of
Samaria and Galilee" (apart from Jericho, the only location he mentions

during the whole nine-chapter journey from Galilee to Jerusalem). When Jesus instructs the ten lepers to "show [themselves] to the priests," two things are implied. First, he is telling them to do what Leviticus instructs those who recover from quarantined skin diseases to do: to get certified by the Temple personnel as cured, so that they might resume normal life in the community. Second, the lone Samaritan (whom we learn later is among the ten) has a dilemma: to which temple should he report? Jesus surely means the Jerusalem Temple, but as a Samaritan he recognizes Mount Gerizim as the true place to worship God and *his* priests are, of course, the Samaritan priests at Gerizim.

Since both Gerizim and Jerusalem are south of Galilee, the Samaritan can begin heading south with the gang of ten, but eventually he must face this choice of the proper place to meet God's mediators. On the way, the ten are cleansed from their disease. The Samaritan, alone among the ten, gets an insight: *neither* Jerusalem *nor* Gerizim is the sacred place to meet the mediation of God's presence. That "sacred space" is now the person of Jesus. And so he comes back to Jesus "praising God in a loud voice." He falls at the feet of Jesus thanking him. There is more to that word "thanking" than meets our English-reading eye and ear. For Luke writes *eucharistōn*—a word that is used in the Greek Bible only for thanks and praise given God. And "God" in Luke's writings is reserved for the Father. Thus, in Luke's language, this sentence is saying, in effect, that the Samaritan is acknowledging that the proper place to encounter the presence of God is in the person of Jesus.

Jesus' own words affirm this insight: "Was no one found who turned back to give glory to God except this foreigner?" Even the Greek word used here for "foreigner" *(allogenēs)* is a tip-off. It was the word used on the signs posted on the balustrade in the Jerusalem Temple precincts separating the Court of the Gentiles from the Court of Israel, banning non-Jews such as Samaritans from that more sacred inner court on pain of death.

Ironically, as Luke will spell out in the Acts of the Apostles, it is the foreigner who comes to see that Jesus is now the privileged "place" to meet the presence and healing power of the God of all.

Twenty-Ninth Sunday of the Year

Readings: Exod 17:8-13; 2 Tim 3:14–4:1; Luke 18:1-8

"Will not God then do justice to his chosen who call out to him day and night?" (Luke 18:7)

MONICA'S PRAYER

That widow in Jesus' parable who kept badgering the judge to vindicate her cause—think of what she was up against. As a widow in the Ancient Near East she is without resources. Since the court of law (the city gates?) was entirely a male realm, we are to picture her as a lone woman amidst a noisy crowd of men. An oft-quoted description of Near Eastern litigation describes a raucous crowd of clients competing for the attention of a judge, who is surrounded by an array of personal clerks. Some clients gain access to the judge by supplying "fees" (bribes) to a particular clerk. The rest simply clamor. The fact that the woman is alone suggests that there is no male available in her extended family to plead her case. She is very much alone in an intimidating situation.

What is more, the judge is described as one who neither fears God nor is he capable of shame before men. Presumably, he is moved only by bribery (the sort of judge implied by Amos 5:10-13), and this woman is either unwilling or unable to use that means. The only strategy available to her is persistence—which finally gets through the irreverent and shameless judge. The more recent New American Bible translation (1986) does justice to Luke's language in describing the frustration of this official: "While it is true that I neither fear God nor respect any human being, because this widow keeps bothering me I shall deliver a just decision for her *lest she finally come and strike me* [literally, "give me a blow under the eye"]." He knows the woman is not going to give up; so he gives in.

There is no question regarding the point of this story. Luke introduces it, after all, by saying, "Jesus told his disciples a parable about the necessity for them to pray always without becoming weary." But if the woman is supposed to be an example of how to pray, why does Jesus take the risk of paralleling God with a godless, shameless judge? This startling way of making a point is an example of what rabbis called *qal wahomer* ("light and heavy")—an argument that reasons in this way: "If it is thus in the 'light' situation, how much more in the 'heavy'?" Jesus uses this ploy elsewhere, for example, in another teaching on prayer, when he asks, "If you then, who are wicked, know how to give good gifts to your children, how much more will your heavenly Father give good things to those who ask him." (Matt 7:11). In other words, if the unstoppable widow can, by her persistence, win vindication from an unjust and godless judge, how much more will your persistence get a response from a loving God?

But if God is, as a matter of fact, *not* a corrupt judge unreachable through appeals to justice and compassion, why the need for persistence? It may be that, from the human side, some situations simply require our involvement in prayer of petition over an extended time. The classic example of this is the prayer of Monica, the mother of the gifted but errant young man that the Church would eventually canonize as Saint Augustine.

In his *Confessions*, Augustine acknowledges that it was the persistent prayer of his mother that facilitated his adult Christian conversion. His description of his own pre-conversion lifestyle portrays what we today may have good reason to identify as a sexual addiction. For example, in book 8, chapter 11, he writes of hearing the voice of Continence saying to him, "Why do you stand on yourself, and thus stand not at all? . . . Cast yourself trustfully on him [the Lord]: he will receive you and he will heal you." His conversion entailed not simply a decision to act differently but a healing from that addiction. Such things take time. In Augustine's case, it required the lifelong prayer of a famously persistent mother.

At this moment in our national history, circumstances involving another gifted and flawed man and another sort of Monica present a kind of epiphany of our national need for healing in a variety of ways. A case can be made that we are seeing patterns of individual and collective addiction—sexual addiction, an investigative and legal process outrunning its original purpose, a practice of partisan politics that is fast losing a sense of the common good, and a media industry and public indulging in frenzied feeding on the whole spectacle. We are hearing calls for a recovery of values, for an enforcement of law, for forgiveness. Each of these calls have their validity. But is it not possible that there is also a deeper call here to a persistent prayer for national healing?

Thirtieth Sunday of the Year

Readings: Sir 35:12-14, 16-18; 2 Tim 4:6-8, 16-18; Luke 18:9-14

> **"He then told this parable to those who trusted in themselves that they were righteous and regarded others with contempt." (Luke 18:9, NRSV)**

How to Justify Yourself

What could be more obvious than the meaning of the parable of the Pharisee and the tax collector? We are presented with a good example and a bad example, and the message comes through loud and clear: Don't be proud; be humble, especially when you pray. That's true enough. But a closer look at the setting shows that most of us, while we get the main point, miss part of the parable's punch because we imagine the setting incorrectly.

Given our North American contemporary experience, it is all too easy to imagine two men praying ("making a visit") in something like an empty church, the Pharisee standing proudly up in front and the tax collector humbly hidden in the shadows in the rear. But that is not the picture at all. When Jesus says that two men went up to the temple to pray, he wants people to picture the Jerusalem Temple, where "to go up to pray" refers not to making a private devotional visit but joining the gathered community in the afternoon atonement sacrifice.

Each man relates to the community worship in a different way. The Pharisee, a member of a group highly respected by most of the community, stands apart from the crowd. The phrase translated "to himself" stands in the Greek between the words for "standing" and "praying"; it makes more sense to relate it to the standing rather than the praying, because praying in this culture was something one did out loud. Thus we are to picture the Pharisee proudly standing apart from the common crowd but not so much apart that some of them couldn't overhear his words.

He begins well enough ("God, I thank you . . ."), but his "prayer" soon degenerates into a proud boast that he is not like other people— thieves, rogues, adulterers "or even like this tax collector." Then he itemizes his pious performances. Whereas the Torah required fasting one day a year, he fasts twice a week (not uncommon among the pious, but conspicuously beyond the requirements of the Law). And, whereas the Law dictates the tithing of *agricultural* products, he gives a tenth of *all* his income. In themselves these practices are commendable, but this Pharisee advertises them, to bolster his pride and to set himself apart from others.

The tax collector, on the other hand, stands apart not in pride but in humility. He beats his breast, and prays simply, "O God, be merciful to me, a sinner." The word for "have mercy" here is not the usual one, the *eleēson* we used to recite at the beginning of Mass, but a rare word, appearing only here in the Gospels, *hilasthēti*, related to words for atonement. Luke's original readers would have caught the resonance. Unlike the Pharisee, the tax collector is fully involved in the Temple liturgy. He is praying, in effect, "Let the atonement work for me, a sinner."

Jesus' concluding words, "I tell you, the latter went home justified, not the former," underscore the context of covenant community. For "justified" means being in right relationship with God, faithful to the covenant relationships. This illuminates the introduction to the story, where Luke says pointedly that Jesus addressed this parable to those "who *trusted in themselves*" (KJV, NRSV, NASB, Rheims) that they were righteous (or justified). In other words, the target of the story is those who foolishly thought their righteousness was based on their own action rather than the grace of God. They placed their faith more in themselves than in God, thereby undermining the foundation of their covenant connections with God and the community.

Our attention to the setting and language of the parable does not change its obvious point, the one stated plainly at the end: "For whoever exalts himself will be humbled, and the one who humbles himself will be exalted." But the setting and language put us in touch with precisely what humbling oneself entails: it is finding one's place in the covenant community, acknowledging one's need for a right relationship that comes only from divine forgiveness. Our own actions do not initiate that covenant relationship. Rather, it is that covenant relationship that calls us to behavior that reflects and acts out our fidelity to those relationships with God and our fellow human beings.

Question for meditation: Is there anything about my own religious practice that could be called self-justification?

All Saints

Readings: Rev 7:2-4, 9-14; 1 John 3:1-3; Matt 5:1-12a

**"Beloved, we are God's children now;
what we shall be has not yet been revealed."
(1 John 3:2)**

POPULATION: 144,000
TAKING APOCALYPTIC SERIOUSLY

As we move toward the end of the Liturgical Year, which culminates with the feast of Christ the King, the Sunday readings grow increasingly apocalyptic. We hear selections from the book of Revelation and also from the part of the Gospels called The Synoptic Apocalypse (Mark 13 and its parallels). The intent is to draw the worshiping community into the perspective of the direction of salvation history, to remind us of the big time-space picture within which we live out our Christian hope. The way we do that this Sunday is to celebrate All Saints, meaning every person, canonized and uncanonized, who is what we hope to become, part of the community in full union with God.

But just when we come to what is most important about our faith, we encounter some apocalyptic imagery that is, for many of us, more puzzling and distracting than illuminating and consoling. What does it mean to take seriously John the Seer's talk about 144,000 saved people, standing with robes washed in blood and holding palm branches? If this is a way of picturing all the saints, how does this way of picturing them help?

There are Christian preachers who insist that to take seriously this image of the saved is to expect that there are literally only 144,000 places in heaven and to make sure that we "make the cut" in that elite corps. To help me visualize what a population of 144,000 looks like, I consult my desktop atlas and discover that 144,000 is less than the population of Lincoln, Nebraska (to pick a nearby site). Put another way, that number is less than twice the number of people that fill Memorial Stadium (76,000) in Lincoln to see the University of Nebraska Cornhuskers play on a Saturday afternoon. Put still another way, within the current population of Earth, figured to be around six billion at the moment, 144,000 is less than three one-hundred-thousandths-of-a-percent. And that is without counting the deceased, who are the only ones who can fully qualify as saints anyway. To make the cut on a team that size, I submit, is about as likely for most of us as qualifying for the defensive line of the Minnesota Vikings.

Fortunately, John the Seer provided some clear clues as to how we are to read this number. The pattern we find in the present reading, an "audition" (something heard) followed by a vision, is something John uses elsewhere to say the same thing two different ways. Thus in Revelation 5 we hear first of an *audition* announcing "the Lion of Judah" and then we are told of a *vision* of a "Lamb standing as if slain." Quite a paradoxical juxtaposition! But both clearly refer to Jesus. What is gained in the startling juxtaposition is the contrast between the Israelite expectation (lion) and its Christian fulfillment (the Lamb). Different, yet the same: the expected lion does in fact turn out to be the victorious, killed but risen, Lamb.

That sets the reader up to understand properly what John presents in our passage. First we are given an *audition* about 144,000 servants of God from all the tribes of Israel, 12,000 from each (with each tribe named in the next four verses, dropped in our Lectionary reading). Then John presents a *vision* of "a great multitude, *which no one could count*, from *every* nation, race, people, and tongue" (emphasis added). Just as in the lion/lamb audition/vision of chapter 5, here we first meet the Jewish end-time expectation and then we see its Christian end-time fulfillment. For an important component of common first-century Jewish expectation regarding the Age to Come was the restoration of the scattered twelve tribes of Israel. The audition that John presents in Revelation 7 is the fulfillment of that expectation—with a fullness expressed in the number 12 squared and then multiplied by a thousand, the big round number of the day, equaling 144,000.

But to ensure that his readers do not mistake a symbolic number for a literal head-count, John then adds to that audition a vision, the picture of a numberless multitude, representing every nation, race, people, and tongue under the sun. Thus the fullness of end-time Israel turns out to be more than Israel. Rather than a limited number, it is countless. Remarkably, our author has also drawn upon the Hebrew tradition to express its surprising fulfillment; for the very phrase describing the multitude echoes the words ("all peoples, nations, and tongues") that describe the extent of the dominion given to the "one like a son of man" in the vision of Daniel 7:13. Just as the lion was announced and the Lamb comes forth; so the restored Israel was announced and the numberless kingdom of the Son of man comes forth.

Thirty-First Sunday of the Year

Readings: Wis 11:22–12:3; 2 Thess 1:11–2:2; Luke 19:1-10

"You overlook people's sins that they may repent."
(Wis 11:23)

LOST AND FOUND

Jesus is shockingly hard on the rich. In the four "Woes" that parallel the four Beatitudes in the Sermon on the Plain (Luke 6:24-26), Jesus categorically condemns the rich. Filled, laughing, and well thought of now, the rich will be hungry, grieving, and weeping. Zacchaeus, the protagonist of today's Gospel, would seem a prime candidate for those woes. Not only is he rich; he is rich in the worst way. He has become wealthy by exploiting his people by collecting taxes for the hated Romans. And he is a *chief* tax collector, meaning that he has profited from the exploitation done by others, the collectors who work under him. Yet the narrative shows he to be one of the New Testament's clearest examples of Christian conversion.

Luke is careful to hint at what it was that opened this man to Jesus' call to a change of heart. Luke says that Zacchaeus was "seeking to see who Jesus was," and that because he was short he climbed up a sycamore tree in order to see Jesus. In describing the man in this way, Luke surely presumes that we have not forgotten what we have read in the passages immediately preceding this account in his Gospel.

Luke 18 is full of talk about the kingdom of God and who gets to enter it. "Amen, I say to you, whoever does not accept the kingdom of God like a child will not enter it" (Luke 18:17). This is immediately illustrated by the counterexample of the rich official who refuses Jesus' invitation because of his attachment to his wealth. This is followed by the famous sayings about the near impossibility of the wealthy entering the kingdom, followed by the hopeful hint that "what is impossible for human beings is possible for God." There follows the third prediction of the passion to the Twelve, who fail to comprehend. Then comes the curing of a blind man who knows exactly what ails him: "Lord, please let me see." To which Jesus replies, "Have sight; your faith has saved you."

With these episodes in the immediate background, we can recognize that Zacchaeus has what the rich ruler (blinded by his wealth) lacked. However ill-gotten his wealth, Zacchaeus has retained a childlike ability to keep seeking the truth. He really wants to see who Jesus is. And "fat cat" though he may be, he has the childlike capacity to take the necessary means to see Jesus: he scampers up a tree to get a better look. When Jesus calls him by name and invites himself into the tax collector's hospitality, Zacchaeus receives him with joy. Predictably, the general population objects to this further example of Jesus' eating with tax collectors and sinners. Zacchaeus shows the effect of this encounter with Jesus by announcing his resolve to amend his ways: "Behold, half of my possessions, Lord, I shall give to the poor, and if I have extorted anything from anyone I shall repay it four times over."

Because that statement is in the present tense in the Greek (reflected accurately in several contemporary translations), some commentators interpret Zacchaeus's statement as a defense of habitual activity and see Jesus' action as standing up for a maligned but decent tax collector. But that interpretation flies in the face of Luke's theme of Jesus' eating with tax collectors and sinners for the purpose of conversion (see Luke 5:32) and the fact that one cannot *routinely* give away half of one's possessions. Moreover, the concluding verses describe what has happened here as an example of the Son of Man seeking and saving "what was lost." The tense of the original text is an example of the use of the present to express resolve (as in, "I'm going tomorrow"). So the translators of our current Lectionary have it right; Zacchaeus is expressing a resolve issuing from a deep change of heart resulting from his reception of Jesus.

Nothing is impossible with God; even a heart toughened by ill-gotten wealth can be changed if there is a residue of childlike seeking and openness.

Thirty-Second Sunday of the Year

Readings: 2 Mac 7:1-2, 9-14; 2 Thess 2:16–3:5; Luke 20:27-38

"[God] is not God of the dead, but of the living, for to him all are alive." (Luke 20:38)

THE GOD OF THE LIVING

The postmodern world speaks with cool rationality about the possibility (or impossibility) of *"post mortem* survival." Some of us review scholastic reasoning about the immateriality of the soul, and others are fascinated with accounts of near-death experiences. New Agers are attracted to Eastern traditions about reincarnation. How strikingly different, in this context, is the biblical approach to life after death. Whereas we are typically drawn either to philosophical analysis or to anecdotal hints from the experience of the dying, Scripture focuses entirely on the covenant relationship with God. This Sunday's readings illustrate unambiguously that biblical approach to life after death.

The excerpt from the dramatic scene of 2 Maccabees 7 provides a vivid example. Forced by the Seleucid tyrant Antiochus IV to violate the Torah (by eating pork) or die with excruciating torture, all seven of the brothers Maccabee die with bold rhetoric on their lips. Notice that their confidence is not something like "You can't really hurt me; I'm immortal." The focus is entirely on their relationship with the Creator—the One who made them in the first place sustains them now, and will reward them in the resurrection of the just. The excerpt in our Lectionary stresses one aspect of that relationship: whereas Antiochus IV (self-nicknamed "Zeus Revealed" [or "Just call me God"]) is, for the moment, king of Judea, the Lord God is king of the world. The Maccabees chose to place their confidence in their relationship with that Higher Power. The whole chapter of 2 Maccabees 7 is worth reading in its entirety; besides providing the gory details of their demise, the narrative presents the powerful words of Mother Maccabee, who reflects that the One who created their lives in her womb is also the Lord of the cosmos, who will surely show his justice by renewing their lives after this horrible death.

Some two centuries after the time of the Maccabees, the Sadducees challenge Jesus on this matter of life after death. The Sadducees, the chief religious authorities among their people at the time, had a very conservative approach to Scripture. They held only to the Pentateuch, the first five books of the Torah. The Prophets and the Writings did not figure in their thought or practice. Since they found no clear teaching on life after death or resurrection in the Torah, they did not subscribe to those Pharisaic doctrines.

Knowing that Jesus did indeed hold for life with God after death, they try to catch him on this point. Attempting to show the belief in the resurrection of the dead is inconsistent with the Torah, they pose the case of a woman who has a series of seven husbands, all of them brothers who marry her when a previous brother dies. This is all done in good order according to the Torah prescription (Deut 25:5-6) that when a man dies without a son, his brother should marry the deceased brother's wife to raise up a son to continue his brother's name. Asserting that resurrection would present the intolerable situation of seven brothers with the same wife, they think to expose the folly of the doctrine of the resurrection of the dead; it is not, in their minds, compatible with the Torah.

In response, Jesus moves right to their proving ground, the Torah, to the passage about the bush in Exodus 3, and draws some implications from the fact that the Lord identifies himself as the God of Abraham, the God of Isaac, and the God of Jacob. Since it would be meaningless for God to declare himself in relationship with persons who have no existence, then Abraham, Isaac, and Jacob must still exist with respect to God. With that rejoinder, Jesus has beaten the Sadducees on their own turf, showing that even their limited canon of Scripture—the five books of the Torah—points to the resurrection of the dead.

All of this reminds us that, even if we are encouraged by reasonings about the immateriality of the soul or the hints implied in near-death accounts, finally our faith in life after death rests on our trust in a permanent covenant relationship with a loving Creator. That puts our hope in life after death in the right place—not in speculations about the structure of human nature but in the revelation about the nature of God.

Thirty-Third Sunday of the Year

Readings: Mal 3:19-20a; 2 Thess 3:7-12; Luke 21:5-19

**"But for you who fear my name, there will arise
the sun of justice with its healing rays."
(Mal 3:20)**

THE SUN OF JUSTICE

As we move toward the end of the Liturgical Year, the Sunday readings continue to sound themes of the end, general judgment, and ultimate salvation. Paradoxically, just when Scripture means to communicate a message of clarity and comfort, we encounter imagery that confuses and alienates many of its readers and auditors. Take, for example, the fire image we meet in the selection from Malachi. When we take seriously Jesus' teaching about love of enemies, picturing God burning up evildoers can pose a problem. At such a moment, we do well to recall Aquinas's reminder that all language about God is a finite attempt to describe the infinite; an image applied to God needs to be both affirmed one way and, in some other ways, denied. The Angelic Doctor made that caveat not to discourage God-talk but to approach such language with care and discernment, minding both what it says and what it does not say. The sun metaphor in today's reading from Malachi is well worth our careful scrutiny.

First, think for a moment about what the sun is for us. In our own, post-Hubble, view of the universe, we know that our sun is one moderate-sized, middle-aged star among many billions of others like it in the cosmos. Even so, we also know, far better than our biblical ancestors, that the sun is absolutely essential to our existence as life forms on planet Earth. All we have to do is consider the lifelessness of our neighbor planets, Mercury and Mars, to realize that we have a privileged relationship with our flaming star. We circle the sun at just the right distance from its heat to receive its light and heat in just the right quantity to be nurtured rather than singed. All life on Earth derives from the energy of the sun. Without the sun, we earthlings simply would not exist. Once we are in touch with this reality, it is easy to understand why many of the world's religions have worshiped the sun as a god.

That realization helps us appreciate why the authors of the Hebrew Bible found the sun an apt *symbol* of its transcendent Creator. Like the sun, God sustains our life, physical and spiritual. Again, better than our ancestors, we know that our sun is the source of the very substance of our planet, which was composed of solar spin-off four and a half billion years ago. So the sun can symbolize God both as originator and as sustainer.

Further, even a child learns early that we have to exercise our human freedom reasonably to relate happily to the sun's fire. If we do not relate appropriately to the peculiar nature of the sun's energy, we can become dehydrated, burned, blind, even cancerous. The same power that nurtures, warms, illuminates, and brings out color can also scorch, sicken, and kill. The difference between our positive and our negative experience of the sun lies not in solar whimsy but in human choices. These aspects of the sun image for God give us a way of realizing how the same reality can be at once "healing" and "punishing."

Paul was making the same point when, in the first chapter of Romans, he spoke of how the apocalyptic "wrath" of God is revealed in God's simply allowing persons to suffer the natural consequences of their disordered actions. God does not burn them; they "get burned" in their violation of the order of creation.

But if the sun works to reflect some aspects of the divinity, it fails in some other ways. The solar image is impersonal and deistic. It could mislead us into thinking of God as unresponsive to human need. That is why the Gospel reading—with all its talk of destruction, insurrections, and persecution—is so encouraging. Jesus mentions these components of the apocalyptic scenario only to insist that these disasters will never finally come between the Lord and his people. "Some of you will be put to death. All will hate you because of me, yet not a hair of your head will be harmed. By patient endurance you will save your lives." How can persons get put to death and still have not a hair on their head be harmed? Only if a caring God sustains them on both sides of death. If the love of God is as powerful, healing, threatening, and awesome as the fire of the sun, it is as protective as the care of a nursing mother. When it comes to talk about God, we need all of the images the Bible has to offer.

Christic the King

Readings: 2 Sam 5:1-3; Col 1:12-20; Luke 23:35-43

"He delivered us from the power of darkness and transferred us to the kingdom of his beloved Son."
(Col 1:13)

KING OF EVERYTHING

Let's face it. For most of us these days, royalty is the stuff of tabloids and talk shows. Ironically, though the print and electronic media were yet to come, things were not much different at the time of the New Testament writers. For the residents of first-century Palestine, and the eastern Mediterranean generally, kings and queens were not a happy topic. For the governed, Herods and Caesars were mainly bad news. And yet, when it came to the long memory and longing hopes of the people of Israel, kings still figured in a big way. God could take an adulterer and a murderer like David and use his gifts of leadership to forge a unified people out of twelve scrappy tribes. And what God could do in a glorious moment of the past, God could do once again in a messianic future, any day now. Whether the current kings of this world were a bane or a boon, the conviction that the Lord God was king of the universe remained the centerpiece of faith.

The kingship of God and the coming reign of God's anointed, therefore, continued to be important in the mind of Jesus and his followers. For that reason, king-talk is still a necessary part of our own language of faith. This Sunday's readings help us recover what we mean when we, tabloid and talk shows notwithstanding, continue to hail Jesus as Christ the King.

The brief passage from the second book of Samuel (2 Sam 5:1-3) is key. It celebrates the moment when the twelve loosely aligned tribes really became a unified kingdom. The elders of the tribes, impressed with David's military leadership, anoint him king and join in covenant union with him. Their sense of solidarity is such that they can say, "We are bone of your bone and flesh of your flesh." In other words, they now claim to be one body with their leader. All this sets a powerful precedent for an image of the end-time king that will emerge later.

Since a popular image of Messiah ("Anointed one" or "Christ") was that of a military savior of the people, it is not hard to understand why Jesus' adversaries would play ironically on the title "king" when they mock him during his crucifixion. In Luke's account of this moment, the leaders jeer, saying, "He saved others, let him save himself if he is the chosen one, the Christ of God." The soldiers taunt him in the same way. In the place for the official description of the crime for which a criminal was condemned to this form of capital punishment, Luke notes that Pilate has posted, "This is the king of the Jews." All of this comes to a head when one of the criminals crucified with Jesus joins the mockery, and the one hanging on Jesus' other side defends Jesus' innocence and then addresses him directly, "Jesus, remember me when you enter upon your reign."

This is a startling act of faith; the man acknowledges that the dying Jesus is indeed a king, but one whose reign extends to the other side of death. Jesus' answer goes beyond the criminal's wildest dreams: "Amen, I say to you, today you will be with me in Paradise." That "today" echoes the "today" of salvation announced at the birth of Jesus (Luke 2:11), in the debut in the synagogue of Nazareth (4:21), and at the conversion of Zacchaeus (19:9—"Today salvation has come to this house").

Later, when Paul wrote to the Christians at Colossae, people surrounded by a culture of Caesar worship, he affirms the vision that Christians, even before death, participate in the kingdom of Christ: "Give thanks to the Father for having made you fit to share in the inheritance of the holy ones in light. He delivered us from the power of darkness, and transferred us into the kingdom of his beloved Son."

Like it or not, the language of our faith commits us to calling Jesus King. We can easily recover what the title meant to our Christian ancestors. Even more important, we know that the question of who has power over us is now and always will be a perennial issue. We pledge allegiance, first of all, to the reign of God in our lives; and that entails hailing the role that Jesus plays in our lives. Gathered in Hebron three thousand years ago, the tribal elders pledged themselves as David's flesh and bone. When we gather at Eucharist, Jesus draws us into an even greater solidarity with his kingship. That has powerful implications for our lives as family members, as coworkers, and as citizens.